PRA

JAMES ALAI

"McPherson was a gifted outlier, and his essays shine with intuitive, canny, unironic, sometimes raw, sometimes disorderly brilliance. This collection, lovingly and incisively curated by the poet Anthony Walton, offers crucial and consistently-revealing resonance to McPherson's luminous fiction."

—RICHARD FORD

"With this superb and timeless collection, one of the great short story writers proves he is also one of the great essayists. Whether musing on the erosion of the black ethos, expressing his unfailing love for his daughter Rachel, or paying homage to his friend and mentor Ralph Ellison, McPherson is at all times the quintessential guide to our moral reclamation. *On Becoming an American Writer* is, in short, a manifesto for our shared humanity, and it's needed now more than ever."

—JERALD WALKER, author of *How to Make a Slave*

"It's a pleasure and a privilege to read James Alan McPherson's brilliant and profoundly beautiful essays. I wish I could send a copy of this extraordinary book to everyone I have ever met—and to everyone I have yet to meet."

—FRANCINE PROSE, author of *The Vixen*

ON BECOMING
AN AMERICAN WRITER

ON BECOMING AN AMERICAN WRITER

ESSAYS & NONFICTION

James Alan McPherson

SELECTED AND INTRODUCED BY

ANTHONY WALTON

BOSTON

GODINE NONPAREIL

2023

Published in 2023 by
GODINE
Boston, Massachusetts
godine.com

LIBRARY OF CONGRESS CATALOGING-IN-PUBLICATION DATA
Names: McPherson, James Alan, 1943-2016, author. | Walton, Anthony, 1960-
    writer of introduction.
Title: On becoming an American writer : essays & nonfiction / James Alan
    McPherson ; selected and introduced by Anthony Walton.
Description: Boston : Godine, 2023.
Identifiers: LCCN 2022016820 (print) | LCCN 2022016821 (ebook) | ISBN
    9781567927481 (paperback) | ISBN 9781567927498 (ebook)
Subjects: LCGFT: Essays.
Classification: LCC PS3563.A325 O6 2021 (print) | LCC PS3563.A325 (ebook)
    | DDC 814/.54--dc23/eng/20220606
LC record available at https://lccn.loc.gov/2022016820
LC ebook record available at https://lccn.loc.gov/2022016821

First Printing, 2023
Printed in the United States of America

To Mary Alice McPherson,
master storyteller and beloved sister.
Rachel McPherson

For Maren.
Anthony Walton

CONTENTS

Introduction

1.

THE HEROIC TRAJECTORY of James Alan McPherson's life is intimated by the headline and subhead of his *New York Times* obituary:

James Alan McPherson, Pulitzer Prize–Winning Writer, Dies at 72

Mr. McPherson grew up in the South, overcoming segregation to graduate from Harvard Law School and become the first black writer to win the Pulitzer Prize for fiction

This short epitaph sets forth an American life that conforms to our desire for Horatio Alger arcs of uplift, stories that allow us to believe in the foundational myths of the nation. In the case of McPherson's obituary, that Alger arc is true, in that it is factually accurate.

Born in Savannah in 1943, McPherson grew up in the South and overcame segregation of the most base, brutal kind to graduate from high school and matriculate at Morris Brown College in Atlanta. As he says in his essay "On Becoming an American Writer," he "left home for college with a single suitcase containing clothes and a National Defense Student Loan" in 1961. But that was only the first leap: he would graduate from Harvard Law School in 1968 and became an acclaimed writer, the author of four books and the editor of several more. He earned tenure at the University of Virginia and subsequently became a beloved, consequential mentor to generations of young writers at the University of Iowa's famed Writers' Workshop. Along the way, he received the Pulitzer Prize (at the age of thirty-five) and a Guggenheim Fellowship; he was in the first cohort of MacArthur "Genius Grant" recipients, and was inducted into the American Academy of Arts and Sciences. He traveled widely, recurrently to Japan, and was the loving father of two: a daughter, Rachel, and a son, Benjamin.

Yet the factual lineaments of McPherson's life do not begin to encompass the story of his life and accomplishments, which can only be measured by a full accounting of his literary—and moral—legacy to the nation, which, from our vantage point, seems a clarion call to acknowledge our greater complexities as human beings and as Americans.

2.

TO BEGIN TO fill in the biographical spaces, perhaps it is best to allow McPherson to speak for himself:

> My brother and I grew up together in a segregated Savannah, Georgia. We had enjoyed a thin cushion of middle-class stability early on, when our father worked as an electrical contractor, the only black master electrician, at that time, in the state of Georgia. But he lost his status, as well as control over his life, before Richard and I were adolescents, and the two of us had to go to work to help our mother take care of our two sisters . . . Richard and I worked very, very hard to get our family off public welfare. In 1961, when I finished high school, I was lucky enough to get a National Defense Student Loan, which enabled me to attend Morris Brown College, a black Methodist School in Atlanta. *(from "Ukiyo")*

At college, McPherson experienced ups and downs, including being bullied, but was able to develop his intellectual gifts, to make his way around the growing southern metropolis, and to exercise his insatiable curiosity about how people in all strata of society lived:

> Between 1961 and 1971, a mere ten years, I had experiences on every level of American society. While in Atlanta, I worked part-time as a waiter at the exclusive Dinkler Plaza Hotel, at the post office, and at the extremely exclusive Piedmont Driving Club (of Tom Wolfe fame)

in Buckhead. During the summers I working as a dining car waiter on the Great Northern Railroad and was able to explore Chicago, St. Paul and Minneapolis, the Rocky Mountains, and Seattle ... I spent my junior year in Baltimore, at Morgan State College, learning about history and politics and literature. After graduating from Morris Brown, I entered the Harvard Law School. I worked there as a janitor, as a community aide in an Irish-Italian Settlement House, and as a research assistant for a professor at the Harvard Business School. In the fall of 1968, I moved to Iowa City, enrolled in the Writers' Workshop, and completed all my coursework in one year and a summer ... I had begun to publish stories in the *Atlantic* in 1968, and I published a book of stories in 1969. *(from "Ukiyo")*

The matter-of-fact unfolding of this narration brings its own pleasure—a boy with no connections leaves a historically Black college and gets into Harvard Law, and then supports himself as a janitor before shrugging off a legal career and lighting out for Iowa City to become a writer—but it also illustrates McPherson's courage. In an unpublished essay, he tells us he began working on the trains while a student because he was broke and had been advised that it was a simple, safe way for a young Black man to make decent money. He found that he enjoyed train work, and it provided the material for his most celebrated story, "Solo Song: For Doc." In addition, he and the future American poet laureate Miller Williams co-edited an anthology of lore, history, stories, and poetry about the American rails, edited by Toni Morrison at Random House.

In the first thirty-five years of his life, it would appear that James Alan McPherson was the embodiment of an ancient Latin proverb: "Fortune is with the bold." It would seem that he had embarked on a campaign to climb and conquer American society. But McPherson was anything but a narcissistic rogue: he was a wanderer. In fact, there are ways in which he could be described as saintly: he was revered by students, praised by neighbors and friends, cherished by family and other writers; after his death, his adopted home of Iowa City named a public park in his honor.

McPherson was highly respected as a person as well as for his writing—an original, a one and only.

3.

THIS BOOK IS intended to provide the briefest of introductions to the essays of this brilliant but under-recognized American author. McPherson's nonfiction resides alongside that of contemporaries such as James Baldwin, Joan Didion, and Hunter S. Thompson, all of whose best work coheres into a kind of prophetic analysis of the ways in which American society would unravel in the latter half of the twentieth century. What distinguishes McPherson from these writers, however, is the astonishing breadth of his frame: He draws from legal, regional, and classical perspectives to give his arguments nuances from contract theory and constitutional law, classical antiquity (Augustan notions of citizenship and Athenian drama, for example), and zones of cultural practice within American life. His vision is both deeply humane and uncannily convincing: some of his notions are novel, others have never been quite so compellingly expressed.

Perhaps the defining trait of McPherson's nonfiction is its concern with what is *moral*—what is *right* and what is *wrong*. He set out to parse carefully and clearly what he thought, making judgments, criticisms, and recommendations. In the 1970s, 1980s, and 1990s, when he was writing these essays, perhaps such moral circumspection was unfashionable, or seen as too earnest, sentimental, even naive—but from our post-Trump vantage point, McPherson's willingness to stare down the corrosive tendencies of American narcissism, untruths, and *mendacity* is a balm indeed.

When McPherson is discussed, much is made of the fact that in 1978 he was the first Black writer to receive the Pulitzer Prize in fiction, which seems, in retrospect, somewhat late for that acclamation to have been settled on an African American, given some of the books that had been published and might have received consideration, such as Jean Toomer's *Cane*, Nella Larsen's *Passing*, Zora Neale Hurston's *Their Eyes Were Watching God*, Richard Wright's *Native Son*, Ralph Ellison's *Invisible Man*, James Baldwin's *Giovanni's Room*, Toni Morrison's *The Bluest Eye* and *Song of Solomon*, and John A. Williams's *The Man Who Cried I Am*. Still, the Pulitzer, is a useful measure of the homeostatic tendencies of elite American literary taste during any particular era, and the fact that McPherson could emerge in 1969 and receive America's highest literary honor less than ten years later is indicative of cultural shifts during that time of social upheaval, as well as recognition of the quality of his work.

It is also enlightening to place McPherson among his generational contemporaries. He can be thought of as the oldest and the first in a wave of canonical Black writers who broke through (with his debut story collection *Hue and Cry*, in 1969), followed in the 1970s by a group that would include Alice Walker, August Wilson, Stanley Crouch, Octavia Butler, Charles R. Johnson, and Gayl Jones. Broadening the pool of his contemporaries beyond African Americans, among his peers were Marilynne Robinson, Steven Millhauser, Richard Ford, Joy Williams, Richard Rodriguez, Robert Olen Butler, Tobias Wolff, Ann Beattie, Paul Auster, David Mamet, Leslie Marmon Silko, and Jane Smiley. McPherson's work not only stands with that of these writers, he was also the first of this broader group to emerge, and this accomplishment should not be overlooked. The older members of this cohort, those born in 1944 and 1945 as well as McPherson, born in 1943, can be described as beneficiaries of the Baby Boom, as they were well positioned to take advantage of the expansion in publishing and educational resources (including MFA programs) that resulted from the postwar economic boom. McPherson, a commercially promoted superstar by his early thirties, a professor in two elite MFA programs, and an artist richly rewarded by the foundation world, is of that changing literary world.

His career, though, might be seen by some as a disap-
pointment, a story of promise unfulfilled. As with many
other Black writers, after his blazing start McPherson re-
ceded into the shadows. Why? we might well ask. Here,
McPherson's gnomic adage "You must not bureaucratize
the numina" suggests one reason. *Numina*, in Latin, is
divine will or the presiding spirit of a person or place;
for McPherson there were sacred aspects of human life
that could not be reduced to procedures and commodi-
ties—many of his essays can be read as a literary artist's
resistance to the demands of fame and the prejudices of
late capitalism.

4.

THE FIRST ESSAY of this collection, "Junior and John Doe,"
provides a bracing introduction to McPherson's manner:
his signature combination of intense first-person point of
view, autobiographical material, historical and social critique, legal insight, and fearless truth-telling, leavened, on
occasion, by wicked humor. He notes that in the 1960s,
many white Americans were deliberately rejecting bour-
geois values while many African Americans were avidly
seeking entrance to the middle class. "My assertion is that
something very tragic happened to a large segment of the
black American group during the past two decades," he
writes. "That is to say, we entered the broader society just
at a time when there was the beginning of a transformation in its basic values . . . In my own view, we became in-

tegrated into a special kind of decadence, which resulted from what has been termed *false consciousness*, one that leads to personal demoralization." Here, we observe McPherson diagnosing the psychological dissonance of two cohorts— white members of the middle class and African American aspirants to the middle class—who were, in that decade, largely moving in opposite ontological directions.

"Junior and John Doe" is followed by another essay, "Ivy Day in the Empty Room," that cuts to the heart of the American racial predicament and particularly to the almost intractable difficulty faced by African Americans. It commences with an almost mocking despair as McPherson describes a conflict between two groups of civically engaged Black citizens in Michigan at odds over the naming of a street in Lansing that included one of the early homes of Malcolm Little, now known as Malcolm X. He writes: "My friend's group wanted a certain street in Lansing named for Malcolm X. The black ministers wanted the same street named for Martin Luther King. I responded to the conflict by pointing out what I considered a bizarre contradiction. At a time when drugs, drive-by shootings, teenage pregnancies, unemployment, self-hatred and racism were decimating whole segments of the group, it seemed of little practical consequence whether a street in Lansing, Michigan, bore the name of either man." But the essay quickly evolves away from bleak cynicism toward an evaluation and reconsideration of the achievement and potential for further inspiration from King, whom McPherson deeply admired. In a profound insight, McPherson links King to what he calls the

American Sacred Language, and its inventor, the Puritan John Winthrop, positing that both men elaborated a similar vision for America, drawing from the Sermon on the Mount in the Gospel of Matthew: "We shall be as a City upon a hill, the eyes of all people are upon us: so that if we shall deal falsely with our God in this work we have undertaken and so cause him to withdraw his present help from us, we shall shame the faces of many of God's worthy servants." King and Winthrop, preaching three centuries apart, both embraced the notion that America was a moral experiment, a test of its citizens' commitment to their professed values.

McPherson evaluates the intersections of religion and race in the third essay, "To Blacks and Jews: Hab Rachmones." First published in 1989, it has even more relevance in contemporary America, given the rise of white nationalists and neo-Nazis. It is a premier example of McPherson's astonishing incisiveness and how his vision leads to truth-telling rarely seen in our public discourse: "Well-publicized events over the past two decades have made it obvious that Blacks and Jews have never been the fast friends we were alleged to be," he writes. "The best that can be said is that, at least since the earliest decades of this century, certain spiritual elites in the Jewish community and certain spiritual elites in the Black community have found it mutually advantageous to join forces to fight specific obstacles that block the advancement of both groups: lynchings, restrictive housing covenants, segregation in schools, and corporate expressions of European racism that target both groups. During the best of times, the masses of each group were influenced by the moral leadership of the elites." It is as if McPherson, speaking to the Blacks and Jews of a generation ago, is also speaking today and pleading with contemporary members of these groups to come together as essential allies.

Whereas he was capable of such sweeping social critiques, McPherson was also a gifted portraitist. "The New Comic Style of Richard Pryor" is a spectacular exhibit of McPherson's dexterity; the profile is a staple of freelancing fiction writers, but it is something he did only once. Written for the *New York Times Magazine* in 1975, the piece is a model of journalistic observation and probity, as McPherson hangs around with Pryor when he was on the cusp of the supernova of stardom that would make him a household name and contribute to his self-destruction and early death. Over the course of several days the two men talk, compare notes on American society, and engage in discussions about racial philosophy and psychology. McPherson notes that his interlocutor deflects certain questions with caginess and a degree of self-protection: "Whenever the conversation reaches a point which requires Pryor to reveal more of his inner self than he would like to make public, he tends either to slip into a character or to laugh. The laugh is a rapid-fire, nervous chuckle, and one can hear within it the footfalls of a perceptive mind backing quickly away from the questioner in order to gauge the depth of the question's sincerity." McPherson's profile is one of the best pieces ever written about Pryor, who had been one of the most important American entertainers in history; it also contains a mini-clinic on the history of American humor, which disguises and, at times, transmogrifies its sources of pain.

"Crabcakes," the next essay, delineates a redeeming cosmic joke played on McPherson himself during a bleak interval in his life. He relates the story of his relationship with an elderly Black woman, Channie Washington, and her family, for whom he served as the oddest of landlords. McPherson stumbled on a house auction that was going to result in the eviction of its poor Black tenants. On impulse born of empathy, McPherson made a bid and won, allowing the family to remain. After the elderly Mrs. Washington passed away, he decided to sell the house. But, as he explains to the reader, Mrs. Washington—with the skill and tact deployed by generations of gentle Black women ferociously intent on guarding their families— convinces him, *from beyond the grave*, not to do so.

The bonds of family—and the uncanny territories into which love takes us—are also prevailing themes in "Disneyland," a profoundly personal meditation on McPherson's relationship with his daughter, Rachel, from whom he was separated by divorce when she was a small child. McPherson refused to lose touch with her, even when he was living in Iowa City and she remained with her mother in Charlottesville. A dedication to fatherhood was a way of addressing a painful lacuna in his own life: "I did not want my own pain, my own bitterness, to affect Rachel . . . like many black males, I had never had a loving bond with a father. The void that this loss left in me was, when I consider it, a kind of opportunity." By means that can only be described as heroic on his part and brave on hers, they were able to maintain a close relationship, a cornerstone of which was regular trips to that most American (some would say most banal) of landscapes, Disneyland: "Perhaps Rachel has seen, in that Magic Kingdom, the places where the rational world, with all its assaults, and the irrational world, with all its potency, meet and dance in some kind of benign compromise about the hidden gods of life and their intentions." Engaging with this most personal of essays brings the reader face-to-face with the terrors, fear, and paranoia of so many Black American parents. We are left in awe of McPherson's attempt to shield his child and create space for her imagination to flourish before it is overrun by the routine, random, and, for a Black child, *racial* cruelties of our society.

In a tribute to another transformative relationship, McPherson's "Gravitas" is a deeply considered remembrance of his mentor Ralph Ellison. Here, the eulogist, in his praise, unwittingly reveals a bit of himself: "He saw himself simply as an American, a product of the complex history of black Americans in this society. He knew that race, and thus racism, was the great obstacle in the emotional and intellectual paths of all black people, but he consistently refused to allow it to overcome him. Both his life and his art were deeply grounded, of necessity, in *agon*. Ralph Ellison was a blues hero." McPherson, in his ironic eloquence, knew Ellison as few others did, and performs the task of illuminating the intellectual scaffolding and achievement of one of the greatest of all American writers. Another feature of this essay is the way that, from time to time, a more socially conservative McPherson comes to the fore; he writes of the grievous wounds Ellison often suffered from other Blacks (such as being regularly catcalled by that most defamatory of African American insults, "Uncle Tom"): "I have had occasion to wonder whether open-admissions programs, black studies programs, and yes, affirmative-action programs have been manipulated by Machiavellians to encourage an anti-intellectual 'third force' made up of envious, narrow, academic hustlers whose only real job is to sabotage those intellectually ambitious black people who just might compete with whites for the good things of the society." McPherson perceived the ways in which African Americans have, at times, undermined one another and discredited some of their greatest achievements.

This "crabs in a barrel" tendency within a minoritized group necessitates, for McPherson, the construction of an alternate and chosen community of friends and neighbors, bound by ideals of *caritas*. In "Ukiyo," which may be McPherson's nonfiction masterpiece, he recounts his life-threatening case of viral meningitis, in 1998, during which he was found unconscious in his home. He subsequently endured a coma that lasted eleven days. Page by page, the essay blossoms into a recursive, patterned reconstruction of the care and responses he received from doctors, nurses, friends, and neighbors, as well as former students, colleagues, community members, travel partners, and long-distance friends. It becomes a moving meditation on human connection, most important the decades-long rift between him and his brother and their subsequent reconciliation, occasioned by his illness.

As if all of that were not enough for one essay, McPherson weaves in an amplifying consideration of the "both/and" thinking that one must embrace to survive and thrive with one's humanity intact in America's racial horror house: "The South, as I had experienced it while growing, and as I had re-experienced it in Charlottesville, Virginia, during the late 1970s and the early 1980s, just did not offer normative opportunities for this kind of human growth. For me, the goal had never been economic success. For me, it had *always* been a matter of personal growth within a communal context unstructured by race. It is a very hard fact of life that there exists no such community in any part of the country. But at the same time, it *does* exist in every part of the country, among selected individuals from every possible background. But this community is a floating world, a *ukiyo*, sustained, incrementally, by letters, telephone calls, faxes, e-mail, visits from time to time. It is not proximity that keeps it alive, but periodic expenditures of human energy and imagination and grace. This is what I have now, as a substitution for a hometown. I find it more than sufficient." He concludes with heartfelt recognition of his prodigal return to his extraordinarily accomplished extended family (including a congresswoman and the first Black pilot of Air Force One), reconstituted after many separate journeys, and their regard and admiration for each other, meeting regularly for enthusiastic family reunions. "Ukiyo" is a celebration of American possibility and a measured accounting of what realizing that possibility can and will cost.

In the penultimate essay, "Reading," McPherson writes an open letter to a book club in Kansas City, relating the story of a teacher who was crucial to his development in her emphasis on the commonplace but essential endeavor of reading, which was not universally encouraged. McPherson notes: "The structure of white supremacy had been so successful that even some of our parents and teachers had been conscripted into policing the natural curiosity of young people. We were actively discouraged from reading. We were encouraged to accept our lot. We were not told that books just might contain extremely important keys which would enable us to break out of the mental jails that have been constructed to contain us. This condition, however, was not absolute." McPherson asserts, in essence, this Emersonian truism: "There is creative reading as well as creative writing," and that for African Americans the self-inventive ethos of both activities is essential.

Finally, in the title essay of this collection, McPherson locates his achievement as a writer inside the larger currents of American society: "I discovered that I had to find, first of all, an identity as a writer, and then I had to express what I knew or felt in such a way that I could make something whole out of a necessarily fragmented experience." For all the difficulty, he never gave up: " . . . I believe that the United States is complex enough to induce that sort of despair that begets heroic hope. I believe that if one can experience its diversity, touch a variety of its people, laugh at its craziness, distill wisdom from its tragedies, and attempt to synthesize all this inside oneself without going crazy, one will have earned the right to call oneself 'citizen of the United States.'" McPherson acknowledges and *embraces* the simultaneous perils and opportunities faced by any American, and proposes his own life experience as one possible model for achieving wholeness in our centripetal society.

What all these essays have in common is a ferocity of thought that organizes itself into a unique, *unprecedented* vision. The more time the reader spends with McPherson's prose, the more it is apparent that he is pushing past common critiques of our society toward a speculative, positive conception of what might come next: "I saw that through the protean uses made of the Fourteenth Amendment, in the gradual elaboration of basic rights to be protected by federal authority, an outline of something much more complex than 'black' and 'white' had been begun." Reading the Fourteenth Amendment, two phrases in particular emerge: "equal protection" and "due process." Thinking about McPherson's childhood and adolescence in Savannah, we can contemplate and understand how he observed those constitutional guidelines *regularly* violated, even trashed, in the daily activities and construct of southern society, and how that witness led him to concepts he would later articulate in his nonfiction.

McPherson utilizes his elite legal education to imagine a moral vision for the future—looking past the Civil Rights Movement of the 1950s, 1960s, and 1970s, past voting rights and affirmative action, to what might come after, what might, from where he wrote, be *possible*: "I do know that early on, during my second year of law school,

I became conscious of a model of identity that might help me transcend, at least in my thinking, a provisional or racial identity. In a class in American constitutional law taught by Paul Freund, I began to play with the idea that the Fourteenth Amendment was not just a legislative instrument devised to give former slaves legal equality with Americans. Looking at the slow but steady way in which the basic guarantees of the Bill of Rights had, through judicial interpretation, been incorporated into the clauses of that amendment, I began to see the outlines of a new identity." This imagining of a new American identity, the prophetic articulation of its possibility, may be McPherson's most urgent gift to us as Americans even if, after Trumpism, its implementation seems ever further away. Yet this is how, through his wanderings, he became an *American* writer with something to teach in the sense that this particular vision, with its underpinnings in both literary history and constitutional law, had not been understood or articulated before.

5.

THE TITLE OF this book is *On Becoming an American Writer*, and embedded in that phrase is a great American story and an African American success story, as McPherson was able, in large part, and unlike so many other Blacks, to fashion a self to *his own* satisfaction. He was able to develop his intelligence, to satiate his many curiosities, and to communicate his findings in luminous prose that limns the early boundaries he was confronted with in ways that transcend them. McPherson wrote in "Ukiyo": "I have now in this house and in my office and in storage close to five thousand books. I left home for college with a single suitcase containing clothes and a National Defense Student Loan." That passage, meant to illustrate how little material wealth the young man possessed when he left Savannah, continues: "But my love for books had grown the more I read and the more I traveled . . . books back then became my life, an extension of myself. They were a necessity for a very special reason. I had been raised in almost complete segregation, had attended a second- or third-rate college, and had been admitted to the Harvard Law School where I had been exposed to the legal and intellectual institutions that governed the country. I had left the law school knowing only two levels of the society: the extreme bottom and, more abstractly, the extreme top. This was still segregation of a kind. Only the experience of reading, I determined, could help me integrate the fuzzy middle areas so I could have a complete picture."

McPherson, of course, became much more than a reader; reading all those books led him to writing, and to the creation of a body of work that not only helped him develop a more complete picture of the United States (and of Japan), but is also acutely original, and, in our current model of national strife, encouraging and helpful to all of us. In his fiction, he was one of the most gifted interpreters of the Black experience; in his nonfiction, McPherson was often looking for a way beyond the morasses in which

Americans find themselves mired. His work is a model of humanistic imagining, an attempt to perform a healing that would, if successful, be the greatest magic trick in American history: to get past race, to help create a singular American identity no longer marred by the existential tragedies of the nation's first four hundred years.

He attempted this profound reimagining of America while remaining immersed in African American history and culture. His achievement demonstrates that an abiding love for Black folks and Black life can rest alongside a mastery of "the King's English" and the desire to be received as an American citizen and participant in democracy. It is time for that imaginative work to be fully comprehended and for this simultaneously American and African American genius to assume a fully recognized place beside the other constitutive voices in our national literature.

Anthony Walton
2022

ON BECOMING
AN AMERICAN WRITER

Junior and John Doe

IN 1961, RALPH Ellison made a prediction. "A period is going to come," he wrote, "when Negroes are going to be wandering around because we've had this thing [the assumption of black American inferiority] thrown at us so long that we haven't had a chance to discover what in our own background is really worth preserving." Nine years later, in an interview, I asked Ellison to elaborate on this prediction. "I think that too many of our assertions continue to be in response to whites," he said. "I think that we're polarized by the very fact that we keep talking about 'black awareness' when we really should be talking about black American awareness, an awareness of where we fit into the total American scheme, where our influence is. I tell white kids that instead of talking about black men in a white world or about black men in white society, they should ask themselves how black *they* are because black men have been influencing the values of the society and the art forms of the society. How many of their parents fell in love listening to Nat King Cole? We did not develop as a people in isolation. We developed within a context of white people."

At the same time that Ellison was responding to me, back in 1970, the polarization began shifting in the other direction as a deadly racial reaction gathered strength.

I remember San Francisco in 1974. This was the time of the Patty Hearst kidnapping, mass hysteria over an impending gasoline shortage, a time when someone named "the Zebra Killer"was shooting white people. At the height of this hysteria, all black males in the city were subjected to an all-night curfew, by order of the mayor, because the "Zebra Killer" was said to be a black male. I used to defy the curfew by sticking with my personal habit of walking when and where I pleased. One night, on a trolley car, a white male holding the strap next to mine leaned close to my ear and whispered, *"This had better stop! It had better stop before we have to go to war!"* Then, changing the tone of his voice, he said "Good night" to me in a friendly manner, and got off the trolley car.

I remember walking one morning to my favorite black-owned restaurant on Divisadero Street. I liked to go there for breakfast. As I approached the place, I saw seated at a table next to the window a black American friend, a writer, and a white male, an Irishman who lived in that mostly black neighborhood and who had a black girlfriend. I went in and sat down with them. While I had never trusted the Irishman because, officially, he was a policeman whom I considered "slick," I had accepted him as the constant companion of my black friend. My friend seemed especially nervous that morning. And the Irishman seemed especially sour and aggressive. I think he might have resented my intrusion. Whatever the source of his irritation, it soon drew my black friend into a ritual that frightened me. As we sat at the table, the white man would occasionally lift his finger, place it before the eyes of my black friend, and move his finger toward some scene or object on the other side of the cafe window. "Look at that," he would order. My black friend's eyes followed the directing white finger, almost as if the two organic objects were connected by an invisible string. "See that?" "Look at that!" "What's that?" The orders came again and again, and at each order my black friend's eyes moved with, or his independent will surrendered to, the authority in the single white finger. This single white finger seemed to be orchestrating my black friend's soul. Afterwards, during this same stressful period, my black friend began speeding up his car, in anger, each time he saw groups of black boys taking their time while crossing street intersections.

It was during the early 1970s that I first began to get a new and curious message from black people. It was then that I first began to hear the word *they* being used in an unfamiliar, self-preempting way, a way that suggested that the pressure of the racial reaction had penetrated and was undermining the value sense, or the private idiom, of black Americans. An early warning came from a friend who had achieved early access to a private club habituated by the white upper class. He gave me some advice he had picked up during his rounds: "*They* saw it ain't go'n' be the way it *was. They* say all this bullshit is *over!*" I next heard this new integration of outside essence into personal idiom from a black colleague in response to my description of homeless black people I had seen on the streets of New York. "Poor devils!" this professor of religious studies said. "Well, *they* won't get *me!*" And the next expression came from a personal friend, a poet who had postured militantly during the 1960s. In response to my account of some very vicious treatment to which I had been subjected by some whites, he said, "Maybe *they* don't like what you write. Don't you understand how much they *hate* you? Why don't you just stand pat and take your blows?" Then there was the black woman who stepped out of the crowd at a reading I gave at the Library of Congress. "They've rewarded you," she whispered to me. "Now why don't you make yourself useful?"

Ellison's prediction did not really prepare me for the counterpolarization of black people during the 1970s and 1980s.

ELLISON'S ATTEMPT TO define a meaningful identity for black Americans came at a time when the attention of much of the nation, if not much of the world, was still focused on the self-assertions of black Americans. His assessments were made during a watershed period, when certain elites still remained poised to redefine the practical implications of the nation's ethical creed in new, other-inclusive ways. A great number of black Americans, those who were then called "integrationists," represented part of the force pressing for a redefinition of the ethical basis of the society. Traditionally, it has always been black Americans who call attention to the distance between asserted ideals and daily practices, because it is the black American population that best symbolizes the consequences of the nation's contradictions. This unenviable position, or fate, has always provided black Americans with a minefield of ironies, a "knowingness," based on a painful intimacy with the cruel joke at the center of the problematic American identity. At the cote of this irony there used to reside the basic, if unspoken, understanding that identity in America is almost always a matter of improvisation, a matter of process; that most Americans are, because of this, confidence people; and that, given the provisional nature of American reality at almost any time, "black" could be in reality "white," and "white" could be in reality "black." Older Anglo-Saxons used to appreciate a few of the ironies in this minefield, or briar patch. They had, in fact, created the circumstances that had given rise to it. When pressed, or when drunk, one of them might tell you in private, "We're all cousins. The only difficulty is that most people don't understand just how we're related."

The fundamental challenge of the 1960s and 1970s was to redefine this special quality of relatedness. The challenge was a simple but complex matter of articulating, or of dramatizing, how the black American idiom, the special flavor of black Americans, was then redefining in its own terms some aspects of the white American essence. This was the subtle, self-affirming dimension of black

American and American experience that could not be comprehended by W.E.B. Du Bois's dualism through its either/or focus. What was needed during and after the 1960s was a creative synthesis, one that would lift the whole issue of black American and therefore American identity to a higher level of meaning based on commonly shared values defined by the experiences of *both* groups. What was needed was a revolutionary model of American identity, an imaginative aesthetic and moral foothold established in the future, with little attention paid to race, toward which all Americans might aspire.

It need not be emphasized that this did not happen.

Because it did not happen, just a few years after Ellison had affirmed his prediction, the minefield of ironies was very suddenly exhausted. Those years marked the true beginnings of the great racial reaction. Stated in terms of tragicomic ritual, or in terms of slapstick, those at the forefront of the charge into the sacred castle suddenly found the drawbridge being raised with most of the invading army still outside. Although no word as harsh as "prisoners" was used, prisoners were indeed taken. They were interrogated in terms of IQ scores, and in terms of the good cop/bad cop ploy of popular melodrama. The "bad cops" (racist social scientists) simply asserted, without any hope of scientific proof, that because of genetic predisposition, black Americans were inferior to white Americans. The "good cops" (sentimental liberals) answered with arguments that black Americans were inferior because of environmental factors. All ironic laughter ceased as this premise was carried forward in the mass media, and all debate about ways to improve the condition of the poor shifted to a discussion of whether or not they are human beings.

Those in the forefront of the movement were stunned, forced now to fight with weapons they had not forged on their own and instead with weapons held within the carefully guarded arsenals of others. The "good cops" won the day, without too many shots being fired. The new black middle class was now isolated from the masses. The resurrected nature-nurture theory had done its work, and was retired to the keep of the sacred castle. Before the experiment in integration, the comic spirit grounded in the realities of the group idiom might have made light of this development with the usual irony. But after Moms Mabley, there was only Richard Pryor to provide the self-affirming communal gestures, grounded in ironic laughter, needed by the group as a safeguard against mechanical or aberrational behavior. Except for the early work of Richard Pryor, during the 1970s reality-based ironic laughter faded out of much black American expression. One result of this was that a large segment of the new black middle class became frightened, conformist, and strangely silent.

Toward the end of the 1970s, I began to hear, increasingly, other-directed allusions being consolidated in our private language. During this period the words *they* and *them* seemed to have become standardized ways of alluding to the relation of our inside world to the larger world outside our group. The old polarity between our idiom and the white American essence seemed to have been thrown into reverse, with the norms of white-middle-class life becoming predominant. Beyond a continuing influence in the areas of sports and entertainment, our private idiom seemed to have lost its capacity to influence the values of the world outside our own. More than this, the passing fashions of the outside world—Du Bois's "tape" of an alien world—seemed to have invaded our very souls. The erosion of something fundamental and sacred began then, and has not stopped since. This great reversal of influences may not have destroyed the group idiom, but it did encourage many of us to allow our eyes to follow a directing white finger; and it did cause many of us to begin to express contempt for poor or unconscious black people who did not know enough to get out of the path of a speeding luxury car.

Sometime toward the beginning of the 1980s, all the "theys" seemed to me to have coalesced into a code of conduct, an acceptable guide to black behavior, the script of which existed outside of the group. This model of acceptable behavior began slowly to function as an internalized norm, causing some of us to begin policing the behavior of others in the group. This new norm was of very special interest to me. I had not realized just how powerful it had become until around Thanksgiving of 1980, when one of my earliest black teachers and his wife visited my home in Charlottesville, Virginia. My former teacher, an elderly man, had a nightmare during his first night in my home. All his life he had been sensitive to the nuances of naked white power. Only such a man could have drawn up into his dreams the unrefined images of white supremacy. On Thanksgiving morning, he reported to me the contents of his nightmare. He said he had dreamed of interviewing a black newspaper reporter who had just covered a top-level briefing of the military high command at the Pentagon. My former teacher reported to me what "they" said: "We should kill a million or so of them, just so the others will understand we mean business and won't start moaning about their 'civil rights.'"

My former teacher was, those many years later, still my teacher. He was prophetic in his expression of the deep fear that invaded the black American soul during the 1980s.

By the first years of the 1980s, I began to appreciate, in a deeply personal way, the consequences of the penetration of this new norm, this new sense of self, into the very core of the black American idiom. I saw the disintegration of whatever sense of self we still possessed. I saw the enthusiastic internalization of the assumed assumptions of "them," and I saw the beginnings of what has become an unending, self-negating, if not self-hating, conformity to the externally imposed model of an acceptable black self. Initially, I took an ironic stance toward this somewhat comic transformation. But when it began to condition the emotional and ethical responses of my family and my oldest black friends, when I saw that white hostility toward me was a signal for black hostility toward me, I abandoned some of my family, and many of my oldest black friends, and accepted a condition of internal exile in a small, isolated town in Iowa as the only way I knew of maintaining myself whole. I accepted this burden of guilt as the price I had to pay for my own psychological freedom. But much deeper than this was my *fear* that the pointing white finger, the one I had observed in San Francisco and in other places, might direct a hostile and inwardly dead set of black eyes at me. For the first time in my life, I began to fear my own people.

Over the past twelve or so years, here in Iowa, I have often wondered whether I might have overreacted in putting great distance between some of my family and my oldest black friends and myself. There is always the temptation, if you are a writer, to be suspicious that your imagination might be overactive. But on the other hand, during these same years I have had to deal with black men and women whom I sometimes considered alien. I have seen a colleague fly into a rage, using the appropriated language of his white peers, over my expression of independent thought. There were too many "theys" in his tirade for him to name. Another acquaintance, when I reported to him the way a black female student had used the bogus charge of racism to browbeat a "liberal" to give her a scholarship, laughed approvingly and said, "She's slick. She'll go far." Like my other colleague, he merely applauded *her* acceptance of the prevailing morality. But the very ease of *both* their acceptances was evidence that something was terribly wrong. Something humanly vital in them had been defeated, and they were involved in a constant process of self-improvisation, an improvisation relying on the "tape" provided by some external script.

I DO NOT believe that Du Bois, or even Ellison, could have anticipated the extent to which black people conformed to the white American model during the 1970s and 1980s. Both their analyses assume a limited absorption of white

influences into the black American idiom. But traditionally, with black people, this reverse integration has
been a highly selective process. Only those traits of the
"other world" that could enhance the group's sense of self
were selected by black people to be incorporated into the
group's ongoing process of self-making. It was only under
a new set of historical circumstances, during the past two
decades, that a large segment of the newly created black
middle class assumed that it had much more in common
with that idealized other world than it had with the vernacular sources of its own vitality.

During these decades, a very large group of black people
took a side trip, so to speak, by attempting to standardize
an identity apart from the concrete conditions of the group
ethos. Many stopped negotiating the complex balance between the moral and aesthetic feeling tones of our own
ethos and the influences, or trends, abstracted from Du
Bois's "other world." Many allowed an assumed corporate
white consensus regarding the nature of reality to predom-
inate over our own instinctive sense of reality. What was
once viewed as a spectrum of choices, some of which were
to be rejected and some of which were to be selected for incorporation because they "fit" (an enterprise undertaken by
any group involved in the process of self-making), became
for many an opportunity to embrace an abstract white-
middle-class model in its entirety. Whereas our ancestors
had abstracted and recombined with great discrimination
and care, many of us accepted unthinkingly the images and
trends paraded before us. In doing this, we won with ease
our centuries-long battle against "discrimination."

But we also disrupted our historical process of making a usable identity, and many of us have settled for a simple standardization around the norms, racist and other, of middle-class American life. One advocate of this standardization is Shelby Steele, who sees something heroic in conformity to middle-class norms. Another advocate is Clarence Thomas, whose story about his rise from the outhouses of his youth *(Up from the Outhouse?)* conforms to the middle-class model of heroism, but stops there. It makes all the difference in the world, at least in the storybooks, whether the hero confronts the dragon or joins him. It makes all the difference in the world what is chosen as the basis of the happily-ever-after. Is it the self-making, self-affirming challenges of the quest, or is it the creature comforts of consumerism and conformity? The issue of race aside, does the basis of ultimate security and identity reside in process or product?

If the answer to this question is the former, then perhaps another, very basic question should follow. What, in the nature of a group ethos, or an idiom, have we managed to bring forward from our failures in the 1970s and 1980s? The visible "leaders" of the group are always bemoaning the fact that we are losing our "gains." But beyond those material things that can be measured, what else, of much greater value, have we lost? I believe that we have lost, or are steadily losing, our sense of moral certainty, the ability to distinguish between right and wrong. I believe that this moral certainty once was, among the best of us, an ethical imperative, one passed along as a kind of legacy by our ancestors. This was our true wealth, our capital. The portion of this legacy that fueled the civil rights movement was a belief that *any* dehumanization of another human being was wrong. This moral certainty once had the potential to enlarge our humanity. Beneath it was the assumption that the experience of oppression had made us more human, and that this higher human awareness was about to project a vision of what a fully human life, one not restricted by color, should be. We seemed to be moving, on an ethical level, toward a synthesis of the "twoness"—the merger of the double self into a better and truer self—that was the end Du Bois had in mind.

Because of the complex ways in which the black American idiom relates to the white American essence, there were certain whites who anticipated the projection of a new *human style,* one which finally transcended race, rising from our struggle. This did not happen. What happened instead was that the process of making a usable identity was minimalized in its ambition: from the humanly transcendent to the material plane, from an ethic based on possibility to an ethic grounded in property. The historical moment had provided us with a choice between continuing a process of human redefinition of an evolving sense of self, with all its pains and risk and glory, and entry into a prearranged set of social formulas. The choice was between process, which is on the side of life, and product, which goes against the fundamental ends of life. Many of us chose the latter option, and something of very great value in us began to die.

While our slave ancestors would no doubt be proud of us as skillfully crafted copies of white people, they would not really recognize many of us as blood kin, as products of the process they initiated. The very first articulation of language in their idiom, as expressed in their songs, had sufficient vitality to look beyond the trends of the moment and identify with an age that was yet to come. The best of them looked back on their own degraded status from the perspective of a future time when their own process of self-making was complete. Denied recognizable human souls by the society that enslaved them, they projected their full souls so far into the future that they became content to look back on their enslavers with laughter, and with pity. This was one measure of their full and self-confident humanity. Where once we shared in their ethical critique of the moral defects in the "other world" of Du Bois's dualism, many of us have now abandoned, or trivialized, this resource. One result of this mass defection is that we now lack a moral center, an independent ethos, a vital idiom. Another result is that the country itself now lacks the moral dimensions once supplied by our critique. It lacks our insights into what is of truly transcendent value. On this essential level of moral abstraction, in those places where *meanings* imposed by the black American group had value far beyond its immediate experience, the group is at risk of losing the catholic dimensions of its ancient ethical struggle for identity.

As a substitute, we now compete with white Americans for more creature comforts. Many of us now eat and dress in extraordinary style. We can lie and lie with greater and greater facility, and can even compete with whites in this enterprise. Back during the late 1970s, the comedian Richard Pryor captured the bleakness of our choice in graphic vernacular language. In one of his routines he portrays a black wino standing on a street corner, humming hymns and directing traffic on a Sunday morning. The wino sees a junkie coming up the street. He says, "Who's that boy? Is that Junior? Look at him. In the middle of the street. Junkie motherfucker. Look at him. Nigger used to be a *genius,* I ain't lyin'. Booked the numbers, didn't need paper or pencil. Now the nigger can't remember who *he* is."

My assertion is that something very tragic happened to a large segment of the black American group during the past two decades. Whatever the causes of this difficulty were, I believe that they were rooted more in the quality of our relation to the broader society than in defects in our own ethos. That is to say, we entered the broader society just at a time when there was the beginning of a transformation in its basic values. The causes of this transformation are a matter of speculation. In my own view, we became integrated into a special kind of decadence, which resulted from what has been termed *false consciousness,* one that leads to personal demoralization.

The basic pattern of this erosion was outlined, early in this century, by the Spanish philosopher Jose Ortega y Gasset, as he contemplated a similar development in his native Spain. "This degradation," he wrote, "merely follows from the acceptance of misgovernment as a constituted norm even though it continues to be *felt* as wrong. Inasmuch as what is essentially abnormal and criminal cannot be converted into a sound norm, the individual chooses to adapt himself to the abnormality by making himself a homogeneous part of the crime weighing upon him. The mechanism is similar to that which gives rise to the popular saying 'One lie breeds a hundred.'"

To fully appreciate the implications of Ortega's insight, one would be required to abandon Du Bois's dualism altogether and view black Americans as simply Americans who, like all others, are open to personal corruption as a consequence of living in a corrupt society. We are required to make the same personal adjustments as others in order to ensure our survival. In this broader sense, the movement of black Americans follows the pattern of other inspired movements to raise the moral tone of an oppressor through an appeal to some transcendent principle. Usually, those armed with only the slogans of liberalism, when they actually confront cynical and entrenched power, reach an impasse. After failing again and again to reform that which is incapable of reformation, such movements tend to regroup in such a way as to leave the sacred ideology intact. Whereas once there was an effort to raise everyone to the same level of equality by pointing to the moral failings of the oppressor, those faced with failure in this tactic often fall back on a much more cynical argument. Since it is not possible to force others to behave as they *should* behave, it is accepted that everyone has the right to behave as the oppressors *do* behave. This leaves the old moral ideology intact as a deadly form of cynicism.

But in the case of black Americans, this cynicism is proving to be much more deadly than the cynicism embraced by other groups. A great many black elites, like

other elites, rushed to embrace the fashionable public behavior of the 1970s and 1980s. Part of the appeal of the
Reagan years was the reemergence of the ideology of extreme individualism—the main chance, the reification of
the bottom line, the location of an ethic in ownership, the
elevation of individual concerns over the common concerns of the group. Many black elites embraced a public
philosophy that helped to justify, for the first time on an
inverted scale, our old "crabs in a barrel" mentality: those
at the top of the barrel should try to *push down* those trying to climb out. This new sense of irresponsible individualism contributed to the growth in the sale of drugs as
the main concern of a new underground economy in the
black community.

And then there was the almost religious identification
with politics. Democratized by Jesse Jackson, a crude political style seeped into many aspects of black American
life. Lying and manipulation in personal relationships
became fashionable. What made these masquerades so
pathetic was the shallowness of the lies and the poor quality of the manipulations. It was as if mentors for the development of these skills had been selected from among
those whites who were themselves on the margins of an
increasingly sophisticated bureaucratic culture. Flabby
tricks seemed to have been learned from those whose own
political skills had become obsolete. This was a product of
our racial marginalization. During the 1980s, whenever I
heard a black bureaucrat depicting with pride the trick
he had used to manipulate toward some end, I silently
compared it with some much more subtle manipulation

I had already witnessed on a much higher level of white society. I imagined this seemingly "new" manipulation as the brainchild of some tired and lackluster white bureaucrat now lost in the mists of time. My silent response was always something like "Crafted by John Doe, Assistant Clerk, Water Works Commission, Cleveland, 1913."

I believe that these preoccupations with fashionable individualism and with small-time politics, toward the end of survival during decadent times, invaded the very centers of our lives. In order to make room for these fashions, we tore down, tossed out, and discarded some of our most basic beliefs. But a very high price was paid for this trade-off. The acceptance of one fashion after another tends to draw the fashionable mind farther and farther away from the sources of its own vitality, its own feeling tones. A preoccupation with public fashions also erodes the unstated values, what the Japanese call "belly language," which provides the foundation for any group consensus. It seems to me that by the end of the 1980s black Americans had become a thoroughly "integrated" group. The trends of public life had successfully invaded, and had often suppressed, the remnants of our group ethic. Our ancient process of self-making had at last found a resting place, a point of consolidation. We were, at last, no better than and no worse than anyone else.

I AM REMEMBERING now a very serious discussion I had with one of my mentors one rainy night in San Francisco many years ago. He had been after me for my usual crime:

speaking my mind to the head of an institution because I thought that what the institution was doing was wrong. My mentor said, "Man, can you afford to *buy* [a certain institution]? Well, *they* can afford to buy integrity a dime a dozen!" After all these years I have reason to concede the truth of my old mentor's assessment. He understood, as I had still to learn, the extent to which ethics and ownership are interrelated in this culture. He was speaking as a learned student of European and therefore American history and culture. And yet I still think he was not quite right. Something happens to the *meaning* of integrity when it becomes a property. It ceases to be an active agent, its value content is cheapened, if not destroyed, and all that remains is an empty fashion. The authentification of such empty fashions by society leads to moral dandyism—a public moral stance or style without private substance. We learn to feign a serious preoccupation with what is assigned value as a current moral fashion, and we learn to view with watchful contempt that which is outside the prevailing consensus of public concern. The result is integrity by consensus, as opposed to the much more willful, much more meaningful kind. It represents the difference between looking outside oneself for clues to what *should* be a current concern and turning within to some private scale of values. It represents the difference between a shifting value sense dependent on outside verification and a value sense that is self-reifying, one that is beyond the control, or the measurement, of time and place. My old mentor was right. Integrity can be measured at a dime a dozen. But the attempt to encase it in material terms, paradoxically, causes it to become even more rare.

Our slave ancestors were familiar with this distinction. Their very lives depended on the ability to distinguish between moral fashions and meaningful actions. They survived by having sufficient vitality of imagination to pass over the present scene, if its currents were not moving in their direction, and identify their meaning with an age that was yet to come. In this way they kept alive the hope of eventually being able to continue moving toward their own goals. In this way a defeated people kept alive a sense of integrity, a sense of self, even if their bodies were bought and sold. During the worst of material times they provided a standard for the best of material times.

I AM PAINFULLY aware that I may be much too critical of negative developments that might have been inescapable for all black people, myself included. I sit here in Iowa City in almost complete isolation from the flow of black American life. My telephone and my letters have provided a lifeline during all these years. On the other hand, I read a great many books and magazines, and I talk on a regular basis with selected friends in other parts of the country. I am beginning to sense that, just now, the group is engaged in a search for something that has been lost. Many of us are looking again to the past. Many of the new middle-class people are trying to fill a void in their lives by embracing a connection between the languages and the cultures of African peoples and our old black

American traditions. Some of our children are learning to salute African flags. There is among us now the belief that, like immigrants from other nations, we must have a homeland to look back on before we can resume the process of making our identity. I have no arguments, now, with the choices being made by others.

But it does seem to me that our slave ancestors resolved this issue many centuries ago, long before most of the immigrants arrived in the United States. In the words of Howard Thurman, our slave ancestors were stripped of everything except what in them was literal and irreducible. Out of this raw and wounded humanity there began to be projected a new people, a people whose only vital lifelines were the roots they planted in the future. All the ancestors who came after them were linkages in the ongoing process of self-making. The present generations are likewise extensions of this same imaginative projection. Many of us have already tried to opt out of this process by attempting to standardize an identity around the norms of middle-class life at a time when the authenticity and the vitality of those norms were questionable. For many, this excursion has proved unsatisfactory. What seems to be gathering strength now is a comparable excursion, this one toward the traditions of ancient Egypt and Africa. Because I am isolated here in Iowa, I think I will sit out this second side trip.

If my years in this place have taught me anything, it is to be even more wary of abrupt shifts in the language and habits that appear around me. I have learned to continue with my own process of making, in my own way. I have learned, mostly on my own, that when the lifestyle out of which the idiom of a people grew is changed or altered, the idiom can break down. Such breakdowns provide the excuses needed to abandon a lifestyle based on a meaning that has been called into question by outside reality. But if the idiom has been identified with the essence of one's own life, and the former lifestyle was merely its transitory expression, then the old values at the basis of the idiom *hold* their essence of identification. Sometimes this holding action can go on for years during a period of readjustment. But afterward it is possible for a *new* lifestyle to grow out of the experience of the old values with a new reality. This is how human beings change with the times while remaining themselves.

What was only an abstraction for me became concrete when I watched the retirement of Thurgood Marshall from the U.S. Supreme Court and the elevation of Clarence Thomas to Marshall's seat. I was interested in Thomas because both of us were raised in Savannah, Georgia, in extreme poverty, and both of us attended schools in the same Catholic system there. When Thomas publicly thanked the nuns in that school system, I could remember names and faces. But as the Senate hearings dragged on, and especially after Anita Hill's allegations, I found myself identifying less and less with Clarence Thomas, as well as with Ms. Hill. Both of them seemed to me to be captives of ideology. At one of the low points in the hearings, after Ms. Hill had testified, my older sister called me from Connecticut. She said, "James, Clarence Thomas didn't attend the same Catholic school we did in Savannah. If he had, he would have remembered the first thing the nuns taught all the kids." And then she recited the first lines of a poem: "I have to live with myself and so, I want to be fit for myself to know."

When the lifestyle out of which the idiom of a people grew is change or altered, the idiom can break down. But if the idiom has been identified with the essence of one's own life, and the former lifestyle was merely its transitory expression, then the old values at the basis of the idiom hold their essence of identification. And afterward it is possible for a new lifestyle to grow out of the experience of the old values with a new reality.

Such a process of continuation and change is an essential part of one's *meaning* as a human being. A reclamation of essential meaning, for black Americans, has very little to do with the other side, the white side, of Du Bois's dualism. But at the same time, considering the white American context of our idiom, it has *everything* to do with it. Once again, we must consider the special interrelatedness of the two groups. Among white Americans, as among black Americans, there is now a desperate hunger for every value once included in the rhetorical category called "ethics." As the responses of "John Doe" to the Thomas hearings must have made clear to a great many people, the current fashion in moral dandyism and lying is about to run its course. The hunger for moral certainties provides much of the appeal of David Duke and Ross Perot. Beneath the open racism of Duke's supporters, one can perceive the first stirrings of a response to the metaphysical problems shared by all people, black Americans included, who have become personally demoralized by living with a false consciousness. For better or for worse, there is now a public lust for moral clarity. This hunger permeates all groups, and transcends the special interests of any one.

I would not advocate a return to a strict religious tradition, but I would hope that the group try again to understand some of the old definitions of the words *truth* and *meaning* and *honesty* and *love* and *integrity*. I am grateful to be hearing, these days, much more familiar language working its way through the black American community: "If you want to talk that talk, you have to walk that walk." I consider this first step toward the reassertion of the old idiom downright refreshing. And I am attempting to consider something refreshingly radical: Since every other attempt at "integration" has failed, perhaps we have one last chance to help each other, through our divided black and white vocabularies, work toward some common and solid definitions.

I want to believe that the spirits of our black ancestors, from the safe perspective of their long-imagined bridgehead someplace in the future, would somehow expect this effort on our part as a final affirmation of the self-definition, the process of making, they initiated those centuries ago. All I have been struggling to say is this: the implication of Du Bois's dualism notwithstanding, we should remember the uniqueness of our origins and locate, within our own idiom, sufficient courage to affirm this uniqueness as the only possible positive norm. Perhaps we should consider doing this as a way of keeping faith with our ancestors. It may well be that the uniqueness of our uniqueness, along with the implications of that, is our most basic value and is the most meaningful asset we have. If so, we ought to find ways of affirming it.

Ivy Day in the
Empty Room

I

ABOUT SIX YEARS ago, at a time when the issues clustered around race still simmered on the back burners of national consciousness, I had a fierce argument with one of my oldest black friends. He had called me from his home in Lansing, Michigan, to report about a conflict between members of his group, people devoted to the memory of Malcolm X, and a group of black ministers who were partisans of the memory of Martin Luther King, Jr. At issue between the two groups was the naming of a street in Lansing, one of the early homes of Malcolm Little, now known as Malcolm X. My friend's group wanted a certain street in Lansing named for Malcolm X. The black ministers wanted the same street named for Martin Luther King. I responded to the conflict by pointing out what I considered a bizarre contradiction. At a time when drugs, drive-by shootings, teenage pregnancies, unemployment, self-hatred and racism were decimating whole segments of the group, it seemed of little practical consequence whether a street in Lansing, Michigan, bore the name of either man. I said that it seemed of greater importance for the two opposing groups to unite their energies to advance the causes for which both men stood and for which they gave their lives. I went further, and enraged my friend, by saying that the worship of the images of these two martyrs, during such a bleak and deadly time, was in reality a substitute for meaningful actions, if not the institutionalization of a death wish. My friend and I broke off our communication after this exchange, and I fell to brooding over whether my response to him had grown out of my own insensitivity to the basic needs, of unsophisticated people, for positive images or role models. Still, the ease with which images were used to obscure substance continued to bother me.

Now, a few years later, the generation of men whose work in early life made the Civil Rights Movement is re-surfacing, though they are radically transformed in terms of public image. Vernon Jordan seems to be a Washington insider. Andrew Young seems to be an elder statesman. James Farmer was on television recently, speaking professorily as a repository of historical memory. John Lewis is entrenched in the U.S. Congress. Ralph Albernathy, after publishing a book describing Martin King as a man of flesh and blood and bone, is dead. Malcolm X has been resurrected, more vital in his martyred youth than he probably was in life, by the cinematography of Spike Lee. To someone who lived through that period of transformation, the re-appearance of such familiar faces brings back memories of what might be called naive optimism about possibilities, both for oneself and for society. There seems now to be a nostalgia for these icons of a Golden Age, a lust for that Sacred Time. But what is missing from this pantheon of heroes is the human image, and the idiom, of the man who was the moral center of the movement they made.

Because Martin Luther King, Jr. has, through a process of iconization or reification, grown larger than life, he tends to exist on a plane far above the everyday concerns of ordinary people. He has been made to function as a caretaker of the Sacred, and any suggestion that he could have ever partaken of the Profane aspects of human life is viewed as something close to blasphemy. His memory has been democratized and fragmented. He lives on street signs, buildings, postage stamps, in biographies, arguments, vilifications. And on his birthday, which is now a legal holiday in every state. During the downside of the winter, a thriving cottage industry of multi-culturalists, diversity sages, merchants of nostalgia, mendicants and sentimentalists reminds us of the details of his life, and of his dreams. These are, for the most part, devotees of Martin Luther King, Jr., the icon, the public figure, mythologized now out of his birthright as a man of flesh and blood and bone.

It seems inevitable that this same process of iconization will also claim, and much more swiftly and efficiently, the man of flesh and blood and bone named Malcolm

X. That aspect of American tradition derived from the ancient Greeks is relentless in its imposition of an ethic, in the case of large-souled men, a mythologizing which ensures survival after death, as one of society's highest rewards. But after the reward has been institutionalized, one basic issue still remains: would the human being at the center of the myth embrace the meaning that has been drawn from his life as the meaning he intended his life to have? Would Jesus of Nazareth, the carpenter's son, accept the version of his life that was filtered through the Greco-Roman perceptions of Paul of Tarsus? Would Martin Luther King, the man of flesh and blood and bone, accept the uses that have been made of his life?

It is useful, while considering this, to speculate about what might have happened if Martin King had not died on April 4, 1968. He was then only a public figure who was already losing the interest of the media. But by 1968 he had begun to oppose the war in Viet Nam and was attempting to form a coalition of the poor in every racial group. Although he might have been less visible during the years after 1968, his support of the anti-war movement might have brought an end to the war much sooner, and his attempt to appeal to the common condition of all the poor might have energized Lyndon Johnson's War on Poverty. Johnson, in turn, might have been able to negotiate a peaceful end to the war that would allow his domestic programs to continue and allow him to remain in office for another term. Robert Kennedy, that other partisan of the poor, might not have been assassinated. And the death of his brother, John F. Kennedy, earlier in the decade, might have been viewed as an aberation instead of as a signal that absolutely anyone in public life—King, Robert Kennedy, Gerald Ford, Ronald Reagan, John Lennon, George Wallace, even Jimmy Carter (and his rabbit)—was vulnerable. These three men, King, Johnson, and Robert Kennedy, might have maintained for a while longer the moral high point of that cycle of history, and might have brought about the necessary transformations in American life. They might have filled, with their voices and through their actions, what has now become an empty public square. We might not have become such a fear-filled people. We might have trusted longer in something larger than ourselves. We might have become much more human.

If such large-spirited men had remained active in public life, perhaps the right-wing reaction, cultivated by Richard Nixon and his silent/moral majority, might not have come to power with such a sense of vengeance in 1968, or 1972, or 1980, or 1984, or 1988. And the sense of security in the public sphere, dependent in large part on continuance at the highest levels of power, might not have been undermined. Moreover, the evangelical idiom employed by King might have become better democratized, but with a meaning that transcended politics. The cause of Civil Rights, which began as a point of entry for excluded minorities into the larger society, might have helped to revitalize the American democratic ethos, as King had intended.

If King had remained active, the status of black Americans might not have remained frozen someplace between desegregation and integration, and the word "integration" itself, which is now in extreme disfavor, might have reclaimed its original meaning, moving from the physical or material plane to an ethical or spiritual one ("Integration is genuine intergroup, inter-personal doing . . . based on unenforceable obligations"); as King had anticipated. We might have tried much harder to become a better people, or at least better than we are now.

Of course, no one man could possibly change the course of a nation of people devoted to a variety of different ends, but King's voice, had it lasted, might have counseled modifications in the means we chose toward those ends. Even if I can now imagine King as only a featured guest on talk shows, answering questions about the current state of "race relations," I am confident that, even in such mundane contexts as "Larry King Live" or "Oprah," he would still be insisting on an ethic that would be a guide to *human* behavior. He would still be speaking a moral language. He would still be speaking confidently about what is *right*.

And as a deeply personal matter, his voice would have helped me to resolve stories that have been stored in my memory for twenty-five years.

April 4, 1968: *My girlfriend, Devorah Watkins, runs into my apartment screaming. She has just heard, in the office of her employer, Robert Coles, the news that King has been shot in Memphis and that riots are beginning in all parts of the country. The Boston police are putting up a blockade around Roxbury, the black section of Boston, while in Cambridge there is the most oppressive silence. We call Devorah's mother in New Jersey. She is crying, too, and keeps saying to me, "Take care of my little girl." I decide to take Devorah to her own apartment on Linnaean Street near Central Square. We leave my apartment with my television set and begin our walk from Harvard Square up Massachusetts Avenue toward Linnaean Street. Ahead of us, in the night, we can see stalled traffic and crowds of silent people. One crowd is moving as a group, a body, seeming to stop and accost other people in cars and on the street. This moving crowd is white. I tell Devorah, "We must keep walking past that crowd. White people are capable of anything! If they try to stop us, I'll throw this television and try to fight them while you run." This becomes our plan. The crowd seems to get larger and larger and whiter and whiter as we approach. We cross Massachusetts Avenue several times to avoid it. Then we are spotted and the crowd crosses after us. Both of us are ready to run when we begin to see, in the streetlights, individual faces. They are all young people, probably students. They follow us and keep saying, as they must have said to individual black people the whole length of Massachusetts Avenue, "We're sorry! We're sorry!" But I am not listening. My mind and my emotions and my imagination have become polarized by now. I am thinking about the police blockade going up around Roxbury. I am thinking, "Suppose they never take it down? Where would I want to be: here in Cambridge, or over there with the majority of black people?" I think and think and think and think all the way to Devorah's place on Linnaean Street . . .*

Twenty-five years later, I still have not resolved this issue.

July, 1968: *My employer, the editor of the Bay State Banner in Roxbury, Massachusetts, has given his permission for me to do a story for the paper on Resurrection City, a sea of tents occupied by representatives of the nation's poor on the Mall, alongside the Reflecting Pool, in Washington, D.C. Because this black paper is poor and understaffed, I pay my own way to the Capitol, and take my own pictures. Martin King has been dead since early April, but a decision has been made by his staff that the long-planned in-gathering of the nation's poor from all groups should proceed as planned. There are many hundreds of tents and many thousands of people, most of them poor, camped out alongside the Reflecting Pool under the brooding, squirrel-hunting, narrow eyes of Father Abraham and the oblivious, blinking red eye of the Washington Monument. Jefferson's statue, off at a distance, is not visible. They have come, the nation's orphans and outcasts, to claim their birthright. They are whites from Appalachia, black people from the South and from the cities, poor farmers from the Midwest, Spanish from the cities and from the Southwest and the West, Indians from their reservations. King is dead, but a nervous spiritual solidarity, something close to hope, remains among them. But a white Park Policeman cautions me to not enter the city. They are savages, he says. They are all poor and angry and looking for something to steal. They may kill me, just to get my camera and my suitcase. And he, the Park Policeman, can provide me with protection only on this side of the picket fence. But my press credentials get me past him and onto the avenues of the vast tent city. Everything around me seems improvised. Ralph Albernathy is there. He*

*is dressed in overalls and is giving a press conference. There
are rumors that he sleeps in a luxury hotel and comes to Resurrection City, dressed for that occasion, only to hold press
conferences. Jesse Jackson is also there. He is sprawled on the
grass, looking elegant in overalls, with a crowd of people clustered around him. He seems to know that a great responsibility is floating in the air, looking for someplace to lodge itself.
He speaks cautiously and confidently to the people around him,
who are mostly black. He says, "Now, if I were to riot and
loot a liquor store, I wouldn't just grab anything. I'd grab the
Chivas Regal . . ." A material age is dawning . . .*

Within a few years, these human beings will be rele-
gated to an abstract category called "the underclass." There
will be few people left with the language to remind us of
who they were, and are. Twenty-five years later, they will no
longer knock on the doors of our imaginations except as
worrisome symbols of homelessness on the evening news.

II

IF MARTIN KING, the man of flesh and blood and bone,
were alive today, if he had not died in 1968, I think that
he would have tired very soon of his ritual appearances on
television talk shows. Like one of his mentors, Mahatma
Gandhi, he might have sought out an alternative forum.
But instead of an ashram, he might have attempted to
re-claim his own meaning from the mythologies that
have been imposed on his life. He might have withdrawn

from enforced obligation to the persona that has grown up around his name, and he might have discovered that the one place where he could truly be centered again was his old jail cell in Birmingham, Alabama. He might have gone there, reflected back on the goals he had set for himself, and measured these against the image of himself, the iconization, that had grown up around his name.

I imagine him looking back over what he had written, and bringing to bear on it the wisdom of maturity and deeper understanding of some of the less admirable, or even tragic, aspects of both human nature and of his own country. I imagine him sifting through his old writings, discarding some ideas and refining others. He might just write another letter, perhaps because that ancient form of communication has also fallen into disfavor. Perhaps this letter would be an open one, addressed to everyone, black *and* white and others, instead of one addressed to only his Fellow Clergymen. Perhaps this letter would begin as his own attempt to reclaim his own basic humanity, his own flesh and blood and bone, from the abstraction and sterility that results from iconization. Perhaps he would go on to generalize, and be much more explicit about, some of the basic moral flaws he criticized in his Fellow Clergymen in his first letter from that jail on April 16, 1963. He wrote then: "One of the basic points in your statement is that our acts are untimely. Some have asked, 'Why don't you give the new administration time to act?' . . . For years now I have heard the word 'Wait!' It rings in the ear of every Negro with a piercing familiarity. This 'Wait' has always meant 'Never.' It has been a tranquilizing thalidomide, relieving the emotional stress for a moment, only to give birth to an ill-formed infant of frustration. . . ." Beneath this language, there might have been a broader criticism, one that his maturity of years might have allowed him to express much more fully. It might be about what happens when a commitment to an abstraction, like "Wait" or "Time," becomes a substitute for meaningful action. This new language might say:

There is in human *nature a nostalgia for perfection. The source of this hunger might pre-exist in the human soul, or it might result from a belief in Democracy as a substitute for a religious sense, or it might derive from the romanticism at the basis of Western tradition. Whatever its source, this hunger for abstract perfection can lead to perverse ends when people, even the most well-meaning of people, give the nerve-centers of their consent, the totality of their value-content, over to the quality of an abstract commitment rather than to the thing to which they profess to be committed. Those who are seduced into this abstract commitment, this idealization, are personally challenged by any reality, outside of this specific ideal, that threatens the purity of their commitment. The perfection of the commitment then, like Ahab's holy pursuit of the white whale, becomes an idol. And the quality of the commitment is viewed as of more importance than the reality of the human community out of which the commitment grows. So Ahab abandons the ship "The Rachel" in order not to be distracted from the purity of his pursuit of Moby Dick. So "liberals" give money to do-gooder organizations so as not to be bothered by the faces and the pleas of homeless people on the streets. So Fellow Clergymen make an icon of Time, and worship it, and avoid learning of what waiting does to Time's victims.*

This lust for unbothered purity of commitment was the focus of King's letter to his Fellow Clergymen. They worshipped the God of Time. But the very same critique might also be aimed at many other groups, who have gained the attention of the public square, in the years since King's death: white and black nationalists, feminists, liberals, paleo-conservatives, neo-conservatives, seekers after middle-class status, environmentalists, even those who sing "We Shall Overcome" on January 18th but who do not speak to black people, or white people, on January 19th. King might even apply this critique to the cult that has grown up around his own flesh and blood and bone. To salvage his own personal meaning from the meaning that has been imposed on his life by the processes of iconization, he might have warned, in his mature years, his own partisans of this tragic mistake: "I make my commitment an idol when the quality of commitment itself becomes more important than the thing to which I am committed."

King might also address himself to the current impasse in the black community concerning the issue of Civil Rights. He might reflect on the reasons why, twenty-five years after his death, the humanly transcendent movement he inspired is still mired in debate over the means toward specific ends; why his beloved community is still stuck in a cycle of desegregation—resegregation—increasing demands for desegregation. During the past twenty-five years of this cycle, advocates of desegregation have been assigned a new category—the Civil Rights Community—and are viewed, sometimes admirably, as creative users of the various laws to break down the racial walls which, somehow, always find ways of reforming themselves—in schools, in neighborhoods, in jobs, and in personal relationships—as soon as the written law looks the other way. The end toward which the strategy of desegration was only a means, integration, has itself become a kind of category, subject to the control of the rule of law.

The entire affirmative action industry grows out of an effort to apply the technology of law to organic human relationships. It also seeks to achieve some balance in artificial human categories, white and black, which are assumed to be natural and unnatural, superior and inferior, privileged and deprived, if not depraved. Moreover, the focus on affirmative action, the legal protection given to oppressed minorities, has led group after group to retreat from association with what used to be called the universals of life and has encouraged the location of the true, the good and the beautiful exclusively within the precincts of one's own category or group. To qualify for this special status, one only need prove, in court, that biology, or life, has made one a victim. Over the past twenty-five years the domain of law has all but replaced, or eroded, personal codes of conduct which once had the potential to create a vital human center, a body of shared assumptions about the commonality of human life in its spiritual precincts. In the absence of such a human center, in situations ripe with spiritual hunger, sects, groups, and ideologies provide substitutes for what used to be assumed as basically human.

Martin King, in his letter from his jail cell in Birmingham, Alabama, seemed painfully aware of the limitations of law as a guide to human doings. He cautioned his Fellow Clergymen: "An unjust law is a code that is out of harmony with the moral law. To put it in the terms of St. Thomas Aquinas, an unjust law is a human law that is not rooted in eternal law and natural law." From his new cell in Birmingham, King might have reflected more on this dilemma. He might have been brave enough to rethink the basic strategy of the entire Civil Rights Movement, which is at the basis of the racial and sexual and group-oriented balkanization of American life.

The Movement itself was premised in the language of American law. Its basic strategy, forcing the American legal system to concede that separate could never be equal, assumed a model of white American society as the norm to which black Americans should aspire. This norm was implicit in the legal attack made by the pioneer of the Civil Rights Movement.

Charles Hamilton Houston, born in the shadow of the Supreme Court's 1896 decision in *Plessy v. Ferguson*, a *Law Review* graduate of the Harvard Law School, the first black recipient of a Sheldon Traveling Fellowship, studied Civil Law in Spain following his graduation. During the 1930s, when he took over the Howard Law School and its students, Houston began to evolve the theories that would lead eventually to a legal challenge of the *Plessy v. Ferguson*, separate but equal, precedent. The Civil Law in Spain that interested Houston was the remnant of old Roman Law. It was what the Romans of the Empire called *Jus Gentium* or *Jus Naturale*, the Law of Peoples or the Law of Nature. That is, the ancient Romans, seeing their Empire consolidated under Julius Caesar and Augustus, evolved a special body of laws, based on the perceived habits of the foreigners in their ports and in their cities, in order to provide legal remedies for their disputes. This body of law was considered natural to *them*, but had no relation to the body of law, the *Jus Civile*, reserved for Roman citizens. The Roman Jurisconsults, who administered the laws, applied one set of "universal" or "natural" laws to non-Romans, and another set of laws, the *Jus Civile*, to Romans. Jurisconsults would not stoop to applying Roman law, the *Jus Civile*, to non-Romans.

In one of history's great ironies, Charles Houston's life-long effort to erode the *Plessy* precedent, which resulted in *Brown v. Board of Education* in 1954, succeeded also in resurrecting, within the framework of the U.S. Constitution, a special set of laws which are comparable to the old Roman *Jus Gentium*. Black Americans, in the almost forty years since the Brown decision, still remain separate, and institutionalized, within the special legal category called "Civil Rights Law." One result is that native-born, multi-generation American citizens, and their basic rights under the Constitution, still remain captive to every shift in the political climate, every modification in the nuanced language of each new political administration. A collective shudder runs through the corporate black community each time a new Justice Department (*Jurisconsult?*) assumes control of law enforcement. *The issue is always whether protection of Civil Rights will be extended once again to foreigners. The issue is never whether the alleged foreigners are in reality U.S. citizens, from many*

generations back, whose basic rights have been in continuous
violation over a period of centuries.

This legal stasis, or limbo, has encouraged a deep cynicism toward the law among black Americans. In the larger
American community, it has contributed to an erosion of
belief in the applicability of "universal" standards within
the context of an American community of citizens equal
under *the same set of laws*, a truly American *Jus Civile.*

One might go further and speculate as to whether this
separate category has become the basis of a new civil religion, with every group which perceives itself as outside the
scope of traditional law, because of biological fate or personal choice, defining itself into *Jus Gentium* and the scope
of its protections. It also raises the question of whether each
new group which claims the virtue of victimization can lay
claim to a special category of legal protections that is much
more valid than the claims that might be made under a
universally applicable common body of laws. If this is indeed the direction in which we are heading, then Martin
Luther King, Jr., the icon, has been elected as High Priest of
the new civic religion named Civil Rights. Also, a brilliant
Constitutional lawyer and former U.S. Supreme Court
Justice, Thurgood Marshall, is being remembered as only
"Mr. Civil Rights." Monuments and museums are steadily
being built to sanctify this special, peculiar status. And the
processes of desegregating streets and buildings, and most
especially minds and spirits, which were once only a means,
have become perpetual ends in themselves.

Meanwhile, while we retreat into a debate over which
group is more victimized and deserving of close attention,

the larger and more important issue remains: just who, even under the purview of the old Roman *Jus Gentium*, remains a foreigner, and what is left of the Romans who maintain the remnants of the old *Jus Civile*? The antagonistic cooperation, the creative tension, between the rule of law and a settled code of conduct, could be ripe with human possibilities. The Americans of the coming centuries will emerge, and mature, out of this tension. According to my own thinking, they will be the ones who act, and who encourage others to act, in areas beyond either a fixation on Civil Rights or on the preservation of the more negative and reductive aspects of the white *status quo*, both of which have produced nothing more than human stasis. They will be the ones who accept the greater challenges and goals of full and equal citizenship, of a higher ethical responsibility towards the human individual, in a space far above and beyond the fires of two radically opposed camps. But after the destruction of most of the country's large-souled men, and during this time of fear, such people, even if they do exist, have no good reason to announce their presence among us, even if they were welcomed.

III

HOMO SUM NIHIL a me alienum puto.
I am a man; no other man do I deem a stranger.

Some version of this phrase has always been at the basis of the professed public values of Westerners, of what was once called Christendom. The Latin ancestral voices of the older cultures have always found subtle expression within the American context. It may well be that our current fixation on the law and on legal processes tends to close out alternate means of achieving desired ends. We are witnessing now a dawning realization of the limitations of the law. The hypothetical "reasonable man" of American jurisprudence now confronts a situation that is much too complex to be open to reason alone. Other cultures admit ethical as well as reasonable voices into their jurisprudence. The Japanese, for instance, admit into their law the question, "In such a circumstance, what would a human being do?" I believe that this culture has now reached a point at which moral models offer much more vitality and possibility of renewal than legal models.

In his last public address, or essay, published in *Playboy* magazine in January, 1969, King attempted to outline what he called "A Testament of Hope." It was fitting that *Playboy* should have been the forum for King's last public words. By 1968, when he died while trying to help garbage men who were on strike in Memphis, King had been all but shut out by the respectable media. The fact that *Playboy* published his last public words, while *The Atlantic Monthly* had published his first, might have confirmed for him the reality of a relation between the Profane and the Sacred.

Almost stripped of all his worldly hopes, King, in the pages of *Playboy*, sandwiched between the nudes and the risque cartoons, offered his insights into what it would take to revitalize a decadent American democratic ethos. "When Rome began to disintegrate from within," he said, "it turned to a strengthening of the military establishment, rather than to a correction of the corruption within the society. We are doing the same thing in this country and the result will probably be the same—unless, and here I admit to a bit of chauvinism, the black man in America can provide a new soul force for all Americans, a new expression of the American dream that need not be realized at the expense of other men around the world, but a dream of opportunity and life that can be shared with the rest of the world. It seems glaringly obvious to me that the development of a humanitarian means of dealing with some of the social problems of the world—*and the correlative revolution in American values that this will entail*—is a much better way of protecting ourselves against the threat of violence than the military means we have chosen. On these grounds, I must indict the Johnson administration . . ."

King died shortly after he wrote this testament.

There has emerged no large-souled black American leader since King because the black American community has learned, very, very well, the price that will be exacted for such principled stands. And yet King did call for, in his last Testament, the emergence of such a moral chauvinism on the part of black Americans. I sometimes think that the black American obsession with material gain, over the past twenty-five years, is only an ironic confidence game. I suspect that most thinking black Americans are really saying, through their actions, "Don't you see? I am only trying to make it. I want to demonstrate my distance from any moral stance that will cause me to be killed. I am not, and never will be, a Martin Luther King, Jr.

And yet we are. And so we name streets after *him*, the better to protect *ourselves*.

Perhaps a fitting resting place for King's legacy, and for his language, should not be within the monuments built to celebrate, or to contain, the spirit of the movement he tried his best to lead. Perhaps he and his language deserve to occupy an integrated room in the national pantheon, a room set aside to honor his basic ethic: "Integration is genuine intergroup, interpersonal doing ... based on un-enforceable obligations." If there ever comes an Ivy Day for those who evolved, and attempted to safeguard, the American Sacred Language, his roommate should be John Winthrop, who laid the spiritual foundations of the tradition that King tried to follow. Winthrop's language and King's language derived from the same sources. Both men renewed the quality of the moral discourse of their day. John Winthrop said, aboard ship, just before landing at the Massachusetts Bay in 1630 essentially what King repeated all during the 1960s:

> Thus stands the cause betweene God and us. Wee are entered into Covenant with him for this worke, wee have taken out a Commission, the Lord hath given us leave to draw our own Articles, wee have professed to enter-prise these Accions upon these and these ends, wee have hereupon besought him of favor and blessing: Now if the Lord shall please to heare us, and bring us in peace to the place wee desire, then hath hee ratified this Covenant and sealed our Commission [and] will expect a strickt performance of the Articles contained in it, but if wee

shall neglect the observation of these Articles which are the ends wee have propounded, and dissembling with our God, shall fall to embrace this present world and prosecute our carnall intencions seeking greate things for our selves and our posterity, the Lord will surely breake out in wrathe against us, be revenged of such a perjured people and make us knowe the price of the breache of such a Covenant.

Now the onely way to avoyde this shipwracke and to provide for our posterity is to followe the Counsell of Micah, to doe Justly, to love mercy, to walke humbly with our God. For this end, wee must be knitt together in this worke as one man, wee must entertain each other in brotherly Affeccion, wee must be willing to abridge our selves of our superfluities, for the supply of others necessities, wee must uphold a familiar Commerce together in all meekness, gentleness, patience and liberality, wee must delight in each other, make others Condicions our owne, rejoyce together, mourne together, labor and suffer together, allwayes haveing before our eyes our Commission and Community in the worke, our Community as members of the same body, soe shall wee keepe the unite of the spirit in the bond of peace, the Lord will be our God and delight to dwell among us as his owne people and will command a blessing upon us in all our wayes, soe that wee shall see much more of his wisdome, power, goodness and truthe than formerly wee have been acquainted with. Wee shall finde that the God of Israel is among us, when tenn of us shall be able to resist a thousand of our enemies, when hee shall make us a prayse and glory, that men shall say of succeeding plantations: the Lord make it like that of New England: for wee must consider that wee shall be as a Citty upon a Hill, the eies of all people are uppon us: soe that if wee shall deal falsely with our God in this worke wee have undertaken and soe cause him to withdrawe his present help from us, wee shall shame the faces of many of Gods worthy servants, and cause theire prayers to be turned into Cursses upon us till wee be consumed out of the good land whither wee are goeing . . .

This is a vision of the Beloved Community that King was trying to create. This was one of the goals of integration. This was one of the sources of the moral language used by Martin Luther King, Jr. It is a language that is in very short supply in these bleak days. If King had lived, he would have made another heroic attempt to reclaim it and to re-apply it to our wounded spiritual circumstances.

This effort to try again would have been the true source of his greatness as a man, of flesh and blood and bone.

To Blacks and Jews:
Hab Rachmones

About 1971, Bernard Malamud sent me a manuscript of a novel called *The Tenants*. Malamud had some reservations about the book. Specifically, he was anxious over how the antagonism between Harry Lesser, a Jewish writer, and Willie Spear, a Black writer, would be read. We communicated about the issue. On the surface, Malamud was worried over whether he had done justice to Willie Spear's Black idiom; but beneath the surface, during our exchange of letters, he was deeply concerned about the tensions that were then developing between Black intellectuals and Jewish intellectuals. I was living in Berkeley at the time, three thousand miles away from the fragmentation of the old civil rights coalition, the mounting battle over affirmative action, and most of the other incidents that would contribute to the present division between the Jewish and Black communities.

I was trying very hard to become a writer. As a favor to Malamud, I rewrote certain sections of the novel, distinguished Willie Spear's idiom from Harry Lessers, and suggested several new scenes. I believed then that the individual human heart was of paramount importance, and I could not understand why Malamud had chosen to end his novel with Levenspiel, the Jewish slumlord who owned the condemned building in which the two antagonists lived, pleading with them *"Hab rachmones"* ("Have mercy"). Or why Levenspiel begs for mercy 115 times. Like Isaac Babel, I felt that a well-placed period was much more effective than an extravagance of emotion. Malamud sent me an autographed copy of the book as soon as it was printed. Rereading the book eighteen years later, I now see that, even after the 115th plea for mercy by Levenspiel, there is no period and there is no peace.

Well-publicized events over the past two decades have made it obvious that Blacks and Jews have never been the fast friends we were alleged to be. The best that can be said is that, at least since the earliest decades of this century, certain spiritual elites in the Jewish community and certain spiritual elites in the Black community have found it mutually advantageous to join forces to fight specific obstacles that block the advancement of both groups: lynchings, restrictive housing covenants, segregation in schools, and corporate expressions of European racism that target both groups. During the best of times, the masses of each group were influenced by the moral leadership of the elites. From my reading of the writers of the extreme right wing, in whose works one can always find the truest possible expression of white racist sentiment, I know that the Black and Jewish peoples have historically been treated as "special cases." The most sophisticated of these writers tend to examine the two groups as "problems" in Western culture. Both share incomplete status. Both are legally included in Western society, but for two quite different reasons each has not been fused into the "race."

Until fairly recently, Jews were considered a "sect-nation," a group of people living within Western territorial states and committed to a specific religious identity. This extraterritorial status allowed Jews to convert and become members of a confessional community, as was often the case in Europe, or to drop any specific religious identification and become "white," as has often been the case in the United States.

This second Jewish option is related, in very complex ways, to the special status of Black Americans and thus to the core of the present Black-Jewish problem. The romantic illusions of Black Nationalism aside, Black Americans have not been Africans since the eighteenth century. Systematic efforts were made to strip Black slaves of all vestiges of the African cultures from which they came. The incorporation of European bloodlines, from the first generations onward, gave the slaves immunities to the same diseases, brought by Europeans to the Americas, that nearly decimated Americas indigenous peoples. The slave ancestors of today's thirty or so million Black Americans took their ideals from the sacred documents of American life, their secular values from whatever was current, and their deepest mythologies from the Jews of the Old Testament. They were a self-created people, having very little to look back on. The one thing they could not acquire was the institutional protection, or status, that comes in this country from being classified as "white." And since from its very foundation the United States has employed color as a negative factor in matters of social mobility, we Black Americans have always experienced tremendous difficulties in our attempts to achieve the full rewards of American life. The structure of white supremacy is very subtle and complex, but the most obvious thing that can be said about it is that it "enlists" psychologically those whites who view their status as dependent on it. It has the effect of encouraging otherwise decent people to adopt the psychological habits of policemen or prison guards.

Given this complex historical and cultural reality most Black Americans, no matter how wealthy, refined, or "integrated," have never been able to achieve the mobility and security available to whites. Jewish Americans, by contrast, have this option, whether or not they choose to exercise it. Blacks recognize this fact, and this recognition is the basis of some of the extreme tension that now exists between the two groups. While Jews insist that they be addressed and treated as part of a religious community, most Black Americans tend to view them as white. When Jews insist that Jewish sensitivities and concerns be recognized, Black Americans have great difficulty separating these concerns from the concerns of the corporate white community.

And yet, despite the radically different positions of the two groups, there has been a history of alliances. Perhaps it is best to say that mutual self-interest has defined the interaction between Blacks and Jews for most of this century. In her little-known study, *In the Almost Promised Land,* Hasia R. Diner has traced the meeting and mutual assessment of the two peoples as presented in the Yiddish press to the two million Jewish immigrants from Eastern Europe and Russia who came to the United States during the first four decades of this century. Community papers like the *Tageblatt* and the *Forward* forged a socialistic language that brought together Jewish immigrants from different backgrounds, that helped them acculturate, and that advised them about the obstacles and opportunities they would find, in America. These papers gave more attention to Black American life than to any other non-Jewish concern. They focused on Black marriage and family, on Black crime, on Black "trickery and deception," and on Black education, entertainment, and achievement. They linked Black suffering to Jewish suffering. Diner writes:

> The Yiddish papers sensed that a special relationship existed between blacks and Jews and because of this the press believed that the two groups were captivated by each other. . . . Jews believed that a history of suffering had predisposed Jews toward understanding the problems of blacks. ("Because we have suffered we treat kindly and sympathetically and humanly all the oppressed of every nation.")

The central theme was that Black people were America's Jews. Historical parallels were emphasized: the Black

Exodus from the South was compared to the Jewish Exodus from Egypt and to the Jewish migration from Russia and Germany.

BUT THERE WERE much more practical reasons why the two groups—one called "white," the other defined by caste; one geared to scholarship and study, the other barely literate; one upwardly mobile, the other in constant struggle merely to survive—managed to find common ground during the first four decades of this century. There was the desperate Black need for financial, legal, and moral support in the fight against racism, lynchings, and exclusion from the institutions of American life. There was the Jewish perception that many of the problems of exclusion faced by Black people were also faced by Jews. Diner writes:

> Black Americans needed champions in a hostile society. Jewish Americans, on the other hand, wanted a meaningful role so as to prove themselves to an inhospitable [society], . . . Thus, American Jewish leaders involved in a quest for a meaningful identity and comfortable role in American society found that one way to fulfill that search was to serve as the intermediaries between blacks and whites. The Jewish magazines defined a mission for Jews to interpret the black world to white Americans and to speak for blacks and champion their cause.

Diner is describing the "interstitial" role, traditionally assumed by Jewish shopkeepers and landlords in Black communities, being extended into the moral sphere. Given the radical imbalance of potential power that existed between the two groups, however, such a coalition was fated to fail once American Jews had achieved their own goals.

For mutually self-interested reasons, I believe, the two groups began a parting of the ways just after the Six Day War of 1967. The rush of rationalizations on both sides— Jewish accusations of Black anti-Semitism, Black Nationalist accusations of Jewish paternalism and subversion of Black American goals—helped to obscure very painful realities that had much more to do with the broader political concerns of both groups, as they were beginning to be dramatized in the international arena, than with the domestic issues so widely publicized. Within the Black American community, even before the killing of Martin King, there arose a nationalistic identification with the emerging societies of newly liberated Africa. In the rush to identify with small pieces of evidence of Black freedom *anywhere* in the world, many Black Americans began to embrace ideologies and traditions that were alien to the traditions that had been developed, through painful struggle, by their earliest ancestors on American soil.

A large part of this romantic identification with Africa resulted from simple frustration: the realization that the moral appeal advocated by Martin King had authority only within those Southern white communities where the remnants of Christian tradition were still respected. The limitations of the old civil rights appeal became apparent when King was stoned while attempting to march in Cicero, Illinois, in 1966. We Black Americans discovered that many ethnic Americans, not just Southern whites, did not care for us. The retrenchment that resulted, promoted by the media as Black Nationalism, provided convenient excuses for many groups to begin severing ties with Black Americans. Expressions of nationalism not only alienated many well-meaning whites; they had the effect of discounting the Black American tradition of principled struggle that had produced the great leaders in the Black American community. To any perceptive listener, most of the nationalistic rhetoric had the shrillness of despair.

For the Jewish community, victory in the Six Day War of 1967 caused the beginning of a much more complex reassessment of the Jewish situation, one based on some of the same spiritual motivations as were the defeats suffered by Black Americans toward the end of the 1960s. The Israeli victory in 1967 was a *reassertion* of the nationhood of the Jewish people. But, like the rounding of Israel in 1948, this reassertion raised unresolved contradictions. My reading teaches me that, until the twentieth century, Zion to most Jews was not a tangible, earthly hope, but a mystical symbol of the divine deliverance of the Jewish nation. Zion was a heavenly city that did not yet exist. It was to be planted on earth by the Messiah on the Day of Judgment, when historical time would come to an end. But the Jewish experience in Europe seems to have transformed the dream of a heavenly city into an institution in the practical world. This tension has turned the idea of the Jews as a nation existing as the community of the faithful into the idea of Israel as a Western territorial sovereign. Concerned for its survival, Israel has turned expansionist; but the price it has paid has been the erosion of its ethical identity. It is said that the world expects more from the Jews than from any other people. This deeply frustrating misconception, I believe, results from the dual premise (religious and political) of the State of Israel. I also believe that American Jews are extraordinarily frustrated when they are unable to make non-Jews understand how sensitive Jews are to uninformed criticism after six thousand years of relentless persecution.

The majority of Black Americans are unaware of the complexity of the meaning of Israel to American Jews. But, ironically, Afro-Zionists have as intense an emotional identification with Africa and with the Third World as American Jews have with Israel. Doubly ironic, this same intensity of identification with a "Motherland" seems rooted in the mythologies common to both groups. In this special sense—in the spiritual sense implied by "Zion" and "Diaspora" and "Promised Land"—Black Americans *are* Americas Jews. But given the isolation of Black Americans from any meaningful association with Africa, extensions of the mythology would be futile. We have no distant homeland preparing an ingathering. For better or worse, Black Americans are *Americans.* Our special problems must be confronted and solved here, where they began. They cannot be solved in the international arena, in competition with Jews.

RELATED TO THE problem of competing mythologies is a recent international trend that, if not understood in terms of its domestic implications, will deepen the already complex crisis between Blacks and Jews. The period of European hegemony, mounted in the fifteenth century and consolidated in the nineteenth, imposed on millions of non-European people values and institutions not indigenous to their cultural traditions. One of these institutions was the nation-state. Since the end of World War II, the various wars of independence in India, Asia, Africa, and elsewhere have exposed the fact that a European invention does not always meet the mythological, linguistic, and cultural needs of different ethnic groups competing within artificial "territorial states." We sometimes forget that it took many centuries for Europeans to evolve political forms suited to their own habits. Since the 1950s, colonized people have begun to assert their own cultural needs. The new word coined to define this process is "devolutionism." While devolutionism is currently a Third World phenomenon, two of the most prominent groups within the territorial United States, because of their unique origins, can be easily drawn into this struggle: Black Americans, because of our African origins and our sympathy for the liberation struggle currently taking place in South Africa; and Jews, because of their intense identification with Israel. Given the extent of Israel's involvement in South Africa, and given the sympathy many Black Americans feel for Black South Africans and Palestinians, it is only predictable that some Black Americans would link the two struggles. My deepest fear is that the dynamics of American racism will force Black Americans into a deeper identification with the Palestinians, thus incorporating into an already tense domestic situation an additional international dimension we just do not need. The resulting polarization may well cause chaos for a great many people, Blacks and Jews included.

I have no solutions to offer beyond my feeling that we should begin talking with each other again.

I remember walking the streets of Chicago back in 1972 and 1973, gathering information for an article on Jewish slumlords who had "turned" white neighborhoods and then sold these homes at inflated prices to poor Black people, recent migrants from the South, on installment purchase contracts. I remember talking with Rabbi Robert Marx, who sided with the buyers against the Jewish sellers; with Gordon Sherman, a businessman who was deeply disturbed by the problem; with Marshall Patner, a lawyer in Hyde Park; and with other Jewish lawyers who had volunteered to work with the buyers in an attempt to correct the injustice. I spent most of a Guggenheim Fellowship financing my trips to Chicago. I gave the money I earned from the article to the organization created by the buyers. And although the legal case that was brought against the sellers was eventually lost in Federal District Court, I think that all the people involved in the effort to achieve some kind of justice found the experience very rewarding. I remember interviewing poor Black people, the victims, who did not see the sellers as Jews but as whites. I remember interviewing Mrs. Lucille Johnson, an elderly Black woman who seemed to be the spiritual center of the entire effort. Her influence could get smart Jewish and Irish lawyers to do the right thing as opposed to the legal thing. I asked her about the source of her strength. I still remember her reply:

> [T]he bad part of the thing is that we just don't have what we need in our lives to go out and do something, white or black. We just don't have *love*. . . . But this ain't no situation to get hung up on color; getting hung up on some of God's love will bail us out. I think of "Love one another" and the Commandments. If we love the Lord our God with all our hearts and minds, and love our neighbors as ourselves, we done covered them Commandments. And "Let not your heart be troubled; he that believes in God believes also in me. . . ."

I think there was, a generation or two ago, a group of stronger and wiser Black and Jewish people. I think they were more firmly grounded in the lived mythology of the Hebrew Bible. I think that, because of this grounding, they were, in certain spiritual dimensions, almost one people. They were spiritual elites. Later generations have opted for more mundane values and the rewards these values offer. Arthur Hertzberg told me, "Anti-Semitism is the way Blacks join the majority. Racism is the way Jews join the majority. Individuals in both groups have the capacity to package themselves in order to make it in terms the white majority can understand."

Certain consequences of the Black-Jewish alliance cannot be overlooked. The spiritual elites within both groups recognized, out of common memories of oppression and suffering, that the only true refuge a person in pain has is within another person's heart. These spiritual elites had the moral courage to allow their hearts to become swinging doors. For at least six decades these elites contributed to the soul of American democracy. Their influence animated the country, gave it a sense of moral purpose it had not known since the Civil War. The coalition they called into being helped to redefine the direction of the American experience and kept it moving toward transcendent goals. With the fragmentation of that coalition, and with the current divisions among its principles, we have fallen into stasis, if not into decadence. Bernard Malamud's Levenspiel the landlord would like to be rid of his two troublesome tenants. I have no solutions to offer. But, eighteen years later, I want to say with Malamud: Mercy, Mercy, Mercy, Mercy, Mercy, Mercy, Mercy, Mercy, Mercy, Mercy

I want to keep saying it to all my friends, and to all my students, until we are strong enough to put a period to this thing.

The New Comic Style of
Richard Pryor

THE HANDWRITTEN SIGN on the door of the modest Hollywood Hills cottage is literary and more than a little self-conscious: "To avoid ill feeling and/or unpleasantness," the sign advises, "please be aware of the fact that uninvited guests are not welcome at any time, whatsoever. To avoid rejection, please do not take the liberty of 'dropping by.' Sincerely and Respectfully, Occupant." On one level of reality, the sign says a simple "GO AWAY!"

Inside the cottage, seated in the living room before a color television set, the occupant at this particular moment is a totally unself-conscious, direct and toothless old blues singer. "Say, boy," he drawls. "Wanna talk to you. Tell you 'bout them fields." The voice is a familiar one. Beneath its drawl, one senses the rhythms of the Mississippi Deltan, the pitch of the South Carolina Geechee, the musical patois of the Louisiana Creole. The face expresses all the wayward experience and wisdom of a full life. As the man talks, the sounds of a guitar and harmonica tuning up flow with the words from his drawn-in lips. "Your mama . . . she a Elk, ain't she? . . . Rode the goat? . . ." Now both the guitar and harmonica sounds fall into place within the lyrics of the old man's song. "Killed a guard in Lou-ez-ze-ana [*whine*]/*Stabbed* him *fiff*teen times [*humm*]/Wouldn't of stab him so much [*whine*]/If he had of been a friend of mine. . . ."

Suddenly the face releases its age, the puckered lips move outward revealing strong teeth, and Richard Pryor permits his real self to appear. "That's one I'm working on," he says, lifting a glass of brandy from the coffee table before him. "When I was a kid in Peoria, he used to sit out in front of Johnnie Mae's Barbecue Pit. The nigger had a goatee, he was toothless, and he had a guitar and a harmonica with tape on the end." Here Pryor mimics the wa-wa sound of a mouth blowing comfortably into a well-worn harmonica. For a moment, he seems to forget he has company as he concentrates intensely on perfecting the technique used by a toothless man playing the harmonica. Finally, he says, "This is it, right? They have their lips sucked in a certain way?" To test the sound, Pryor begins to improvise with the voice, evoking a scene in which a bashful-sounding but obviously cunning Southern black man is trying to underestimate his skills at playing dice in order to outwit a group of Northern black men. "Oh, I gambles a little," the voice says. "Me, I a'mit that. Say, now, the two green ones I had befo', you ain't changed them now, did you? God-*dang!* 'Cause I know y'all slick up here." What becomes visible in Richard Pryor's face and audible in the old man's voice is a complete understanding of the assumptions which once structured social relations between Southern and Northern black people. Across the room, next to picture window, small human faces laugh and applaud on a television game show. The sound is turned down. Richard Pryor dissolves his comic mask, looks at the television and laughs back. "Mercy?" he calls into the next room. "Bring me a pair of socks."

"Long ones?" his housekeeper, Mercy, answers from the back of the house.

"Yes, ma'am," he says.

A very proper Chicano woman brings the socks. Pryor puts them on and leans back on the sofa, sipping his Courvoisier. He is an ordinary-looking honey brown-skinned man, with a thick Afro and a thick black mustache curving downward toward the edges of his lower lip. The face gives the impression of never being comfortable enough to come to rest inside itself. His manner is almost shy. "I'm waiting to watch 'Zoom,'" he says about the silent television. "It's one of my favorites, along with the cartoons."

DESPITE HIS PRIVATE manner, Richard Pryor is one of the most popular comedians of his generation, although he is largely unknown to the broad American public. Almost singlehandedly, he is creating a new style in American comedy, a style that some of his admirers have called "theater" because there is no other category available for what he does. His style relies on extremely subtle dimensions which must be observed and heard at the same time in order to be completely understood and appreciated. Indeed, there is no way his brand of comedy can be described in writing without the generous use of parentheses noting nuances in sound and facial expression. Mel Brooks, one of his admirers, has called him a comic of "*outré* imagination." *Rolling Stone* magazine has said that Pryor's comic style is "a new type of realistic theater," a theater which presents "the blemished, the pretentious, the lame—the common affairs and crutches of common people." Most black audiences love Richard Pryor. He appears before them at night clubs and in concerts, and there are occasional glimpses of him on television and in movies. But because of the particular nature of his art, because of the materials on which he draws, Pryor will probably have great difficulty reaching the wider white public. Unlike most comedians, his comedy is heavily visual; and also, unlike most comedians of his caliber, Pryor cannot utilize television in his search for broader audience.

The cause of his exclusion is Pryor's choice of materials. The characters in his humor are winos, junkies, whores, street fighters, blue-collar drunks, pool hustlers—all the failures who are an embarrassment to the black middle class and stereotypes in the minds of most whites. The black middle class fears the glorification of those images and most whites fear them in general. Pryor talks like them; he imitates their styles. Almost always, he uses taboo words which are common in their vocabularies. And he resists all suggestions that he modify his language, censor his commentary. As a result, Pryor's audiences have been limited to those who attend his night-club and concert engagements. These are mostly black people. When he does appear on television, it is only as a guest; and even then he is likely to say something considered offensive to a larger and varied audience.

Although his routines seem totally spontaneous, his work has moved away from the stand-up comic tradition employed by comedians like Lenny Bruce. Pryor improvises, but his improvisations are structured, usually springing from within his characters. He seldom throws out one-liners just to haul in laughter, unless it is social commentary leading to the depiction of a character. Instead, he enters into his people and allows whatever is comic in them, whatever is human, to evolve out of what they say and how they look into a total scene. It is part of Richard Pryor's genius that, through the selective use of facial expressions, gestures, emphases in speech and movements, he can create a scene that is comic and at the same time recognizable as profoundly human. His problem is that he also considers certain aspects of their language essential to his characters.

"I couldn't do it just by doing the words of the person," he says. "I have to be that person. I see that man in my mind and go with him. I think there's a thin line between being a Tom on them people and seeing them as human beings. When I do the people, I have to do it true. If I can't do it, I'll stop right in the middle rather than pervert it and turn it into Tomism. There's a thin line between to laugh with and to laugh at. If I didn't do characters, it wouldn't be funny." Here Pryor pauses. "When I didn't do characters, white folks loved me."

There are many whites, however, who do admire Pryor. Like his black audiences, they seem to recognize he has completely abandoned the "cute" and usually paternalistic black comic images of the sixties, popularized mainly by Bill Cosby. Pryor's people are real and immediately recognizable by anyone who has had contact with them, whether in a black skin or a white one. He does not allow them to get away with anything. If it is true, as Henri Bergson has suggested, that laughter is a corrective, a social gesture that has as its purpose the punishment of rigid or inelastic conduct, Richard Pryor is giving a public airing to some of the more unadmirable styles of the urban black community and making his audiences recognize them for what they are. Any good comedian can do this, but it is Pryor's special genius to be able to make his audiences aware that the characters, though comic, are nonetheless complex human beings. "Watching Richard perform," said *Rolling Stone*, "is like watching yourself and all victims of human nature on stage; it can be painful and it can be exhilarating." The magazine call this new comic style "the theater of the routine."

If "routine" means the passions and pains of ordinary people, Pryor definitely qualifies as an interpreter. His life has been rich in experiences which have allowed him to observe such people. He was born on Dec. 1, 1940, in Peoria, Ill., the stereotyped center of Americana. He says that his family ran whorehouses. His grandmother, a New Orleans Creole and a Catholic, was the owner. All kinds of people, including politicians, came within the range of Pryor's perception.

But possibly the strongest influence on him was his father, who, Pryor hints, was that very complex kind of black man given to operating by his own rules and within his own sense of reality ("Cut this stuff short!" Pryor recalls his father saying to the priest at his mother's graveside, while holding back tears. "It's cold out here!").

Pryor attended Catholic school, receiving all A's, he says, until the business activity of his family was discovered and he was expelled. Transferred to public school, he was put into a class for the mentally retarded because of his hyperactivity, and remained in classes for slow learners until his expulsion in the seventh grade for hitting a science teacher. Before he left school, however, a teacher encouraged him to act in skits at a local community center. In the meantime, he also hung out on the corner and worked in a packing house.

His career as a comedian began in the Army and continued, after his discharge, in small clubs in Peoria, East St. Louis, Youngstown and Pittsburgh. In the early sixties, he worked his way east to Greenwich Village and Borscht Belt clubs in the Catskills, developing his abilities as an improviser. His materials at that time reflected the country's preoccupation with integration. Pryor admits to being influenced during this period by an early record by Lenny Bruce, probably the classic "I Am Not a Nut, Elect Me!" on which Bruce came as close as he ever would to making the transition from strict commentary later made by Lily Tomlin and Pryor. But Pryor's chief model at this time was Bill Cosby, who was the first black comic to reach a broad white audience. Pryor imitated Cosby, he says, because a white agent told him that Cosby was the kind of black man white television viewers would not mind having in their homes.

In the middle sixties, Pryor began appearing on the Ed Sullivan, Mery Griffin and Johnny Carson shows, and eventually started working before predominantly white audiences in Las Vegas. During this period, he married and divorced several times, made a sizable amount of money and developed a habit for cocaine. In 1970, he says, he experienced what might be called a breakdown on the stage of the El Aladdin Hotel in Las Vegas. He says he became frustrated because he felt the current of characters developing inside his head and could not "go" with them, restricted as he was to the expectations and tastes of a white night-club audience. He walked off the wrong end of the stage, leaving Las Vegas and encouraging predictions that he would never again hit the big time.

IN 1972, HOWEVER, Richard Pryor surfaced again, this time in the role of Piano Man in the movie "Lady Sings the Blues." The comedian who had attempted to locate the comic vein in largely white audiences had been replaced by an actor capable of very subtle interpretations of his characters. In "Craps After Hours," Pryor's second recorded album, he returned to the people and the comic situations he knew intimately. He still did commentary, but his approach was altogether different. Instead of remaining aloof from his characters, Pryor became them, moving beyond interpretation to total integration of himself and his materials.

Later, he played dramatic and comic roles in six other movies, including "Hit," "Wattstax" and "Uptown Saturday Night." He wrote scripts for "Sanford and Son" and Flip Wilson, and, in 1973, helped write two television specials for Lily Tomlin. He won an Emmy award for this work. During the same year, he worked with Mel Brooks on the script for a movie tentatively titled "Black Bart," which became the highly successful "Blazing Saddles." In 1974, just before the movie opened to mixed critical reviews and wide audience acceptance, Pryor was indicted for failure to file income-tax returns on $250,000 earned between 1967 and 1970. After plea bargaining, he was fined $2,500 and sentenced to 10 days in jail.

Shortly afterward, his third recorded album, the X-rated "That Nigger's Crazy," was released; it promptly sold a million copies. He resumed making personal appearances, this time before predominantly black audiences, in San Francisco, Detroit, Harlem and Washington, D. C.

Returning to Los Angeles after months on the road, Pryor now seems determined to make another attempt to reach movie audiences, only this time not as a writer or a supporting actor. This time, he is writing his own film script, "This Can't Be Happening to Me." The sign on the door of his home, as well as his calm deliberation, suggests that he will allow nothing—hack work, fans or interviewers—to interrupt his concentration on the script. Though he watches television in the late afternoon, the set runs without sound; and he will talk to a guest only until it is time for "Zoom" to come on.

RICHARD PRYOR DOES not like to analyze his work, but he seems to have come to some firm conclusions about himself, his audience and their standards. "I don't know what I do," he says simply. "I know what I won't do. I don't know what I will do. I turned down big money because I won't work Vegas and be that type. [Here he mimics the sound of a band playing a hackneyed introductory chord: da de dah dah, da de dah dah . . . 'Hi, folks,' the nervous voice of a standup comic says. 'Gosh, what a pleasure. . . .'] I trust my audiences now. I worked the Apollo in Harlem. I was scared to death. Them niggers will eat you up if your shit ain't right. But they responded and I was fine after that, wherever I went. I worked Detroit, Chicago—every place the same. People felt good. And to see people laughing at each other and not being so serious, that made me feel good. The record people tell me now they can release my old work. I say, 'You can't release nothing, not under my name. You underestimate them people that bought my last album. They didn't buy that to make me a million seller; they bought it because they liked it. And as long as I keep them liking, they'll buy. And when I stop, they won't.'"

He drinks from his Courvoisier and glances at the television before continuing. "The Mike Douglas Show" is progressing in silence. "See, there's a spotlight, and whoever stands under it, it don't matter to nobody. But I'm going to do mine right. Whenever they say, 'Richard Pryor,' they can trust me. Whenever I do a movie, I want them to say, 'Starring Richard Pryor? I'm gonna see that 'cause know Richard Pryor gonna make us laugh. Bring the family!' There may be some blue words in it—they don't care. It's going to be funny."

What Pryor describes as "mine" is his ability to absorb and then re-create the lifestyles of the people around him. "I be listening to dudes talking, all over," he says, "in whorehouses and places. Everybody be talking the same kind of talk. No matter what city you go to, it's the same feeling, a universal feeling. That's what they be laughing at, themselves. They see themselves when I do a character. I noticed going around working for black people who're in depression now, they all laughed at the same things wherever I was working. There's a kind of unity. In different cities, wherever I am, they be laughing at the same shit, so I know we all know what's happening. I say. 'Well, now, Huey [Newton] done went crazy. Whipped his tailor 'cause the pants was too long.' And they laughed all over 'cause they knew who I was talking about. They knew about all the niggers who died following after him, and here he is beating up a tailor."

Most people, black or otherwise, would find it difficult not to respond to some of the characters of Richard Pryor's humor. Among them are a philosophical wino who hands out advice to passersby, including Dracula and a junkie; the denizens of an after-hours joint; a meek blue-collar drunk who picks his weekly fight in a barroom, is beaten, then goes home to his wife bragging that he will make love to her, only to fall asleep; a pool shark named The Stroker; a braggart named Oilwell who showers policemen with muscular rhetoric; a white policeman named Officer Timson; a whore named Big Black Bertha; black preachers, hillbillies and assorted minor characters—all of whom have individualized qualities. Not one is a stereotype. Their scenes are introduced from within them and conform strictly to the patterns of their individual experiences. Pryor presents them with such thoroughness and fidelity to their speech, gestures, flaws and styles in general that the same characters are recognizable to audiences in all parts of the country. Pryor's characters are human, and only that.

Even hillbillies tend to recognize themselves in Pryor's routines. "They'll come up to me," he relates. "They'll say, 'Man, I'll tell you. I mean that was really funny.' It's a strange feeling that transcends all that other stuff. They'll say, 'I know a guy just like that.' They mean it. You can see love for that guy in their faces."

It is significant that Pryor has considerable difficulty explaining this phenomenon. Instead, he slips easily into the character of a hillbilly, as if he would allow the man to explain himself. One recognizes immediately the truck driver, the service-station attendant, the man occupying the adjoining seat on the Greyhound bus, the lonely man on the next stool at the lunch counter. There is the smile with just a bit of condescension, the slightly conspiratorial eyes, the lips pulled in tight against the teeth, the nervous hitch in the shoulder signifying, perhaps, an uncomfortable intimacy. "Wal, buddy," the voice says, "you know that

reminds me of the time Jed Tudd and I—we uz daawn in
El Paso—" the voice is flat and nasal, with just enough
hesitation and hurry to suggest a friendly tension—"and
a old boy—I never will forget this—see, we uz loadin' manure on the back of a truck, and these boys come speeding
down through there, and they just hit them brakes. God-
dam, what a time! Just shit spread all over the highway. . . ."

No ONE REALLY knows what makes us laugh. Henri Bergson theorized that the causes of laughter are external to
ourselves, though existing within the context of what is
human because laughter is dependent upon others for its
echo. We know that we laugh at mechanical gestures, rep-
etitions, inflexibility of character or language—any rigid-
ity behind which we can perceive something human. To
Bergson, laughter is a corrective which punishes the mechanical in human behavior. Freud sought for the source of
laughter deep inside the chaos of man's unconscious self—a
self from which, Freud said, the comic spirit erupted occasionally in a release of powerful impulses. These are two
of the theories, but the source of laughter is still a mystery.
    As Americans, we tend to laugh because laughter cre-
ates the illusion of unity and ease, when in fact we have
never been unified or at ease. We laugh at the comic
masks behind which we all hide in our endless searches
for individual identities; for by laughing at the masks, we
can laugh, with more emotional ease, at ourselves. This is
why, as Constance Rourke has pointed out, the whole of
the American comic tradition has been one of social crit-

icism. And vernacular humorists, from Mark Twain and the great political cartoonists to the best stand-up comics, have depended on an earthy level of language to provide resonance to their criticisms.

Viewed from the perspective of this American tradition, Richard Pryor is the first totally unself-conscious black comic to turn his perceptions—and language—on black people themselves. He forces them to look at their faults and laugh. Assured of their humanity, he holds up before his audiences patterns of behavior which have evolved into somewhat rigid styles, and reminds them that they are only masks—and comic ones at that. His audiences laugh with him because they too know they are human.

Only Pryor knows his audiences well enough to do this. Only he could have made them laugh at the escapades of Huey Newton. Pryor's character Oilwell spouts bragga-docio at policemen: "I'm Oilwellll, 6-foot-5, 222 pounds of mannn!" It does not matter that Oilwell is beaten up by the policemen. What matters is that Pryor's audiences can laugh at Oilwell's pretensions. When Pryor is onstage, his audiences shout, "Do Oilwell! Do Oilwell!" They have seen his style over and over. It has become mechanical and therefore comic.

In a Detroit theater recently, Pryor recalls, two black policemen came to his dressing room and reported they had just arrested a black suspect who used a line introduced by one of Pryor's characters in a comic routine: "I-am-rea-ching-into-my-poc-ket-for-my-li-cense." According to Pryor, one policeman said, "Don't you bring that to me! What you trying to do, a routine? Richard Pryor? Well,

I'll do my part. Spread your cheeks! Put your face on the ground!" Then both policemen and the suspect stood there laughing with and at each other.

Pryor does not relate that anecdote without stating his ambivalence toward policemen. "They made me nervous," he says. "I was raised to hate cops. I'm sorry. We ran a whore-house, and I was raised to not trust police. I know we need police, 'cause there are some niggers that'll pull the truck up to your house, and say, 'Give the furniture up! No, we's taking the furniture!' No, we need police. It's the police that you don't need that's in the way. But for these policemen to come to me was nice. And they liked me. See, the human-ism in them hadn't been lost; it's just the job they had to do."

Part of Pryor's own humanism turns on the way he uses the word "nigger." His comic scenes are sprinkled liberal-lywith this gem, so much in fact that some black people have complained he is damaging the image of the group by moving the word from the pool halls and barber shops back into public usage. The word "nigger," however, has never gone out of style. The movie industry and some whites op-posed to busing have done far more than Pryor to keep the word alive. Also, and more important, there is a significant difference between Pryor's use of the word and the way it is used by whites to evoke an abstraction. When Pryor says "nigger," he is usually about to define a human type in all his complexity. It is to his credit that he is able to start with an abstraction and make it into a recognizable human being. If he does his work well enough, it would be difficult for even the most offended listener, white or black, not to say, "I've seen this man before."

WHENEVER THE CONVERSATION reaches a point which requires Pryor to reveal more of his inner self than he would like to make public, he tends either to slip into a character or to laugh. The laugh is a rapid-fire, nervous chuckle, and one can hear within it the footfalls of a perceptive mind backing quickly away from the questioner in order to gauge the depth of the question's sincerity. But in matters touching his humanity, Pryor does not laugh and he speaks for himself. "It's love for them," he says. "I don't think you could do impressions of somebody you hate. If it is hate, it's some kind of admiration for something: the worst in the best, and the best in the worst."

He nods at the silent television. On the early evening news, there is a feature about Los Angeles people who visit homes for retarded children and the elderly. A mentally retarded white girl is on camera. "How do you hate that?" he asks. "'Cause she's white? You wish that on her?" A little black boy is bouncing a basketball to entertain a group of elderly white people. "Look at them old people," he says, "that old man sitting up there." The old man is smiling. The little black boy is smiling. "How do you hate that? 'Cause it's black? I wouldn't want to be like that. Can you imagine the hearts of people all tied in hatred?"

As an example of what hatred does to an individual, he offers his own insights into the psychology of the white guards he observed while serving his 10 days in prison. He talks of how hate can extend into a guard's family life and affect his children. Step by step, he traces the psychological devastation from prisoner to guard to wife and children to the community. His descriptions are accurate and sobering. Then, to break away from this line of conversation, and to do so without laughing or slipping into a character, Pryor says, "Hey, has anybody ever written Santa Claus in June? Say, 'Dear Santa, how you doing? You all right, man? Here's a scarf. Wrap up. I know it's cold up there. How's the wife and kids?' Nobody thinks of that," he says. It is obvious that he is now eager to see "Zoom" and the cartoons.

WHAT IS IT at the basis of Richard Pryor's comic style that enables him to enlarge his characters even while we laugh at them? Recognizable immediately are the speech styles of the "boys on the block," black preachers, blue-collar workers, policemen—all the types likely to be found in urban black communities. But when introducing them in comic scenes, Pryor does some very subtle things with their language. Expressed within the sounds of certain words are ideas which help define each character and expand the comic situation. The pomposity of a black preacher is suggested by the extra emphases on certain words ("I first met God in 1929," Pryor's preacher says, "outside a little hotel in Baltimore . . . and the voice got magniff-ficent and whooly and re-zoundedah"). The egotism of the character Oilwell rings through the broad sound of his self-definition ("I'm Oilwellll, 222 pounds of maannnnn!") The intransigence of a street-corner tough is incorporated into his lingo: "I ain't goin' nowhere. He go'n to mooove me!" (The idea of a pushing contest is incorporated into the sound "mooove"; it expresses resistance to forced removal.)

Richard Pryor is very sensitive to such subtle shadings of pitch and inflection. "Niggers just have a way of telling you stuff and not telling you stuff," he observes. "Martians would have a difficult time with niggers. They be translating words, saying a whole lot of things underneath you, all around you. That's our comedy."

But Pryor's sensitivity to verbal nuance is only one aspect of his comic style. The most important aspect, the one that makes his routines theater, is the almost unbelievable mobility of his face. His is probably the most expressive comic face since Chaplin's. It can express hundreds of subtle moods with very rapid shifts, making it impossible to see where one shading ends and another begins. Where did he acquire this skill? Pryor does not mind disclosing that he got it at the movies. "Cartoons are the art form of the movie industry I learn most from," he says. "They can do such things with cartoons. They can say such heavy things. Life now is a cartoon. We are cartoons."

Perhaps Richard Pryor is right. He is a child of the American movies, especially the animated-cartoon branch of it. Among the major movie influences on his comic style, along with Jerry Lewis, Fuzzy Q. Jones, Red Skelton, Pat Butram, Smiley Burnette and Abbott and Costello, Pryor lists Porky Pig, Bugs Bunny, Baby Huey, the Roadrunner, Mickey Mouse and the Little Rascals. As a youngster in Peoria, he spent many Saturdays watching matinees featuring as many as 25 cartoons, most of which accelerated the movements of humanlike animal forms by synchronizing them against up-tempo music. After more than 20 years, Pryor's face is trained to not miss a single beat in its union with the rhythms of his characters' speech. In his mind, he has integrated frame after frame of emotional nuance demonstrated by cartoon figures as they encounter seemingly insurmountable obstacles. In the forties and fifties, they were mere cartoons. In 1975, they seem much closer to the reality we see around us.

The final dimension of Richard Pryor's comic style is a moral one. Mel Brooks has said Pryor possesses "almost Nietzschean ideals of what is good, what is powerful, what is superior." While contributing to his humor, these same standards prevent Pryor from taking himself too seriously. He will not, for example, accept invitations to speak to young black kids about the dangers of drugs because of his past involvement with cocaine. "I feel like a hypocrite," he says. "As much cocaine as I snorted. The kids know that; they ain't stupid. All I can say to kids is, 'Know what you want to do.' I can tell them there ain't nothing happening in jail. You'll die, or be treated like a dog. If that's what they want, fine. I can't stop it."

Still, one senses that his imagination is drawn to the victims of drugs and that he has the most profound sympathy for such people. Because he must look, and because his imagination is essentially comic, he arranges what he sees, no matter how horrible, into comic patterns. He speaks of Harlem, of having seen there three blocks of junkies in Army jackets waiting under yellow lights for their contacts to arrive. His face registers the most profound sadness. In trying to describe the scene, he assumes, unconsciously, the voice of a movie director, and then the voice of an Army sergeant directing the movements of the junkies and their contacts: "Ten-hut!" he barks. "Roll up sleeves! Tie-off! Cookers-on! Ready-needles! Shoot-huh! Nod-huh! . . . ."

FOR ALL OF its appeal, Richard Pryor's comic style is not for everyone, although, watching him portray a character in a comic scene, one realizes that Pryor's people have always existed. In Elizabethan England, a period with a lower class whose manners and styles resembled some of those found in urban black communities, Oilwell might have been called Pistol, Big Black Bertha might have been called Doll Tearsheet or Mistress Quickly, the boys on the block might have been named Bardolph, Peto, Gadshill and Poins. There might have been a sly old man, curiously resembling Redd Foxx, with the name Jack Falstaff. During that period, a genius who knew all levels of his society made a place for them in his historical plays. He produced great drama. Richard Pryor's is a different kind of genius. He knows intimately only one level of his society. But at least he is reminding us, in his special kind of theater, that such people still exist.

Watching Richard Pryor in front of his television, one senses that he is weighing very carefully the cost of his resurrection as a comic and the options now open to him. When "Zoom" comes on, he turns up the sound and sings along with its theme song. Mercy, the housekeeper, brings in hamburgers. Pryor says, "Thank you, ma'am." Then he looks at the television screen and says, "Kids' laughter, don't it mess with you? They're so natural. They ask, 'Why?' That's the greatest kid question in the world, 'Why?'"

He studies the screen again. "I know all the tricks," he continues. "I assume that everybody does. But people like me because I won't use them, and if I do they can tell. I ain't never done that, and if I keep my pace I ain't never gonna be like that. I do like to work on television, but they say, 'No, we have to have laughter in there.' I say, 'Don't you think people are sophisticated enough to enjoy something without being told when to laugh?' The laughter is in yourself. If you don't want to laugh, you don't have to laugh, you could just be enjoying something. You don't have to laugh because somebody in the audience is laughing."

He finishes his hamburger quickly, looks around and smiles, and suddenly grabs part of a hamburger from the plate of his guest. It is a kind gesture. It says, I want to be friendly, but I also want to be alone. The gesture is much better than Pryor's exploratory laugh, and more gracious than his slipping into one of his characters. Richard Pryor is a young man from the streets of Peoria—a man whose skills have proved themselves marketable. He is also a keeper of the comic spirit for at least one level of American society. He may yet find ways to expand the range of his experience and the range of his responsibilities.

Crabcakes

SEVERAL WEEKS AFTER the call from Elizabeth McIntosh, and my response to it, the letter from Mr. Herbert Butler arrives.

> Dear Mr. McPherson,
>   I am doing fine. I want to thank you for your card, letter and kindness during (my) the loss of my beloved Channie. She is with the Lord now . . .

Mr. Butler has crossed out the initial "my," his personal claim to Mrs. Channie Washington, and has instead generalized her death into a significance greater than his own loss.

His use of "the" implies acceptance.

I am glad that Mr. Butler is in this frame of mind. I am glad that he is open to acceptance of loss. I have clear fee simple in the house he now occupies. Mr. Butler was never the official tenant. Mrs. Washington was the person who sent the monthly rent. Although she never signed an agreement, there existed an essential understanding between the two of us. Mr. Butler was always in the background of our private, unwritten contract, as he was always in the background of her monthly letters to me. I have no bond with him.

I have decided to sell the house. I now intend to take the profits I have been avoiding all these years, and be rid of my last connection with Baltimore. A friend in Washington, D.C., has already put me in contact with a real estate agent in Baltimore, and this woman has already made an appointment to see me. I have already begun preparing, by the time his letter arrives, just what I will say to Mr. Butler: For almost eighteen years, I have not made one cent of profit on this house. I have carried it, almost on my back, at great loss. You must remember that when I purchased this house back in 1976, I lowered the rent to eighty-six dollars a month. Over the years, I have raised it only enough to cover the rise in property taxes. After seventeen years, the rent is still only two hundred dollars a month. Repairs, fire insurance, ground rents—all these additional expenses I have paid for, over all these years, out of my own pocket. Now I am tired of, and can no longer afford, so many scattered responsibilities. I must cut my losses now and try to consolidate. You, Mr. Butler, will have to go. But there are homes for senior citizens, with nurses on call and with organized activities for elderly people. Meals will be regular, healthy, and free.

I have already checked into them for you. There will be a private telephone by each bed, free heat and electricity, family and visitors can come and go freely at almost any hour. In such well-cared-for places, the furnaces always work in winter. Mr. Butler, you will be more comfortable, and maybe happy, in such a new home. Now, in this old place, you have nothing but memories to comfort you, or to haunt you. The change I am suggesting is probably, when you really think about it, a good thing. You should take some time and think carefully about it, Mr. Butler. I am not setting a deadline for you to go.

My plan now is to work on this speech and make it right.

It is essential that Mr. Butler understand my point of view. I am no longer affluent enough, or arrogant enough, to do for anyone else what the state could more easily afford to do. I do not plan to be ruthless. I will only disclose my intentions to Mr. Butler. The real estate agent, Ms. Gayle Wilson, will handle the hard part. As soon as she finds a buyer, she can handle the eviction. I will not have to get involved. No one could possibly blame me. I have already done more than enough for them. Their needs have become infinite, while my own surplus has shrunk. Mr. Butler will have to see the motif in my narration. It is the old story. Perhaps Mrs. Washington's death was, paradoxically, heaven-sent to bring the story to its end. Both Mr. Butler and I agree that she must be in heaven now. It may well be that the end her death brought to the story was her final letter to me.

Over close to eighteen years, I calculate, Mrs. Washington must have sent me almost 208 letters with her rent checks.

I remember some of them.

I go through the boxes of letters received this year and find several from her. I inspect them and see now, for the first time, that the very last letter, sent the first week in this month, is not even in her handwriting. I sense this, but take care to check this last letter against the handwriting in the one that arrived with the September rent. This one is in Mrs. Washington's hand. It is her uneven writing, her flow of sentences without periods. I read it carefully and notice something unfamiliar. She has written "Dear James Family" instead of her usual "Dear James and Family." Also, there is a line that is completely new, something I have never seen before in any of her monthly letters. This new line is: "I will close my letter but not our love . . ." This new language seems strange. It suggests an intimacy that has never existed between us. It also suggests a finality that frightens me.

Mrs. Washington seemed to have known, back in early September, that she was about to die.

But I dismiss this thought. Besides, her profession of unending love is inappropriate. Mrs. Washington did not know me in that way. She knew only a few facts about my life. She knew that I once lived on Barclay Street in Baltimore, two blocks away from the house in which she lived. She knew that I made my living as a teacher. She knew that I was married. She knew that I moved from Baltimore to Virginia, and she knew that after two years I moved to New Haven. She knew that I moved back to Virginia for two more years. And she knew that I moved then to Iowa. Her monthly rent checks and letters followed me to these new addresses. I never wrote back to her and offered any more details about my life. I did visit her in Baltimore from time to time, to see about her and the needs of the house. But for almost eighteen years the facts of my own life have been kept from her, while the facts of her life have been hidden from me by the standard phrases in her monthly letters. These phrases have not varied in 208 months: "Everything is fine." "Thank the Good Lord." "May God bless you all." "May God be with you all." "Thank the Good Lord For every thing." I wonder what the new owner of the house would think about the letters wrapped around her monthly rent checks, if Mrs. Washington were still alive to write them. Then I think about its future sale.

Then I begin to remember the sweating, hungry heat of the crowd.

I begin to remember.

I begin to imagine and remember.

An Old Portrait in Black and White, July 1976

TWO ELDERLY BLACK people, a man and a woman, sit on a porch in a tarnished metal swing. It is the porch of a rundown red-brick row house. The swing, under their weight, is straining against the rusty chains suspending it and swaying back and forth. The two people are sitting in the swing on the porch of 3114 Barclay Street in Baltimore. It is a weekday, but they seem dressed in their Sunday best. The woman wears a white necklace and matching white earbobs. She is smiling as if it were indeed Sunday morning and she is lost in the sermon of a church. An otherworldly serenity, or perhaps a childish inability to appreciate finely textured reality, is in her smile. She looks wide-eyed from behind large spectator eyeglasses. But the man looks, from a distance, sheepish and embarrassed. He wears a gray touring cap pulled down close to his eyes. His belly rises up from behind his belt. There is a this-worldly awareness in his fat brown face. Other people, white, move through and out of the screen door of the house. They slide behind the couple on the swing, jostling windows, knocking on the fragile woodframes, scraping new rednesses into the worn bricks. Others move up and down the gray concrete steps or mill about on the sidewalk. A white auctioneer is standing on the top cement step speaking rapidly and abstractedly to all questioning newcomers. His dead eyes always focus on a space above their heads. He has the ritual assurance, the slow, sure movements, of a priest. Parked and double-parked along Barclay Street, glistening in the wet, hot morning sunlight, are tail-fin Cadillacs, wide-reared Buicks, Oldsmobiles, Fords, and Chevrolets—the nests of middleclass army ants. From a distance, from across Barclay Street, the entire scene, with the house at its center, seems too restless to be real life. It looks speeded up in time, like an animated cartoon. Framed as the slow-moving backdrop of such relentless restlessness, the two black people seem frozen in time. They look like stage props, brought by mistake onto the wrong movie set. An awareness of this error seems to be in the old man's face. The old woman seems to see secret amusements in the show. As the priestly auctioneer opens the bidding, time seems to flow backward, as if a hidden director now realizes his mistake in the staging of the scene. *This is not Barclay Street*, something is reminding. It is a public square in Virginia, South Carolina, Georgia. It is 1676, 1776, 1876, *not* 1976. The relentlessness of the ritual has only temporarily sucked open black holes into the flow of time, opening a portal into a finished past that has come alive again and oozed out and forward, into the future. Soon it will move back to where it was freeze-framed dead. Something in the air assures this coming correction of the scenery. This is why the two black people are so passive. This is why the white auctioneer seems so abstracted. The milling crowd, too, is restless for correction. The weight of ritual has pushed their roles too far back in time. *The portal into the past must close.* All—the crowd included— have found unholy meaning in the slipshod staging of this moment. All are looking from far back into what will be and from the here and now back on what was only *then* inevitable. The reflections in the life-linked mirror belie all notions of age and elevation and change. Time is not a circle. What was was, before *was* was?—the answer to the puzzle *should not be* "is." No matter that in Virginia,

South Carolina, and Georgia such people always wore their best clothes, *someone,* at a distance from the crowd, thinks. This is not Virginia or Georgia or South Carolina. It is 1976. It is the celebration of the Bicentennial. *Someone* moves from the other side of Barclay Street and through the lines of cars and into the crowd. He moves close just as the auctioneer opens the bidding. It is anger that now makes his voice heard above all the others. It is arrogance, too, *but also something else,* that causes him to make a stand within the circling centuries on the hot morning sidewalk. *What was that thing? What became of that something else? The* white auctioneer chants his mass. It is anger, and also arrogance, that causes *someone* to match each bid and raise by five hundred dollars. The blood sport flowing through the crowd begins to slow and ebb. Its forward motion is arrested by a single collective thought: this *must* be some trick, some sly rhetoric left over from the public bluster of the past decade. Time can prove promiscuous on such hot days. *But what if there is no bluff and the price keeps rising?* The collective voice falls into weak and individualized efforts at continuing combat. The heat in their blood begins to flow backward, into the past, while time hurries forward first to apologize and then to make its correction. The white auctioneer points disinterestedly and mouths the sacred incantation: *"Sold!"* The circle breaks. The black hole closes. The mirror looking out and in from hell is cracked. Time flows like clockwork, forward, while the crowd mills. Those who are most nimble speed off first in their cars toward the next house on the list. The auctioneer holds his hand out for a cash deposit. The balance is to be secured by mortgage in three days. He keeps his hand held out, like a kindly priest reclaiming the chalice from a slow communicant. *This is my body. This is my blood.* Now someone walks up onto the porch and kisses the forehead of the old black woman on the swing. She says, *someone remembers now* that she said, "You must be from up *there?* The woman, close up, looks even more serene and on vacation from this world. The old man seems ashamed. But the woman seems to be smiling for both of them. Someone says to her, *not to him,* "You won't have to move now. You can live here for as long as you want. No matter what you are paying now, the new rent will be eighty-six dollars a month." The view, facing Barclay Street from the old porch, is now unobstructed. The last of the wide-reared cars, the habitats of army ants, are leaving. It is a wet, hot summer morning in Baltimore, July 1976. The auctioneer, in his short-sleeved shirt, is sweating while he waits on the top cement step, away from tire comfort of the porch.

I recollect now that day and that time.

It was not a public square in Virginia, South Carolina, or Georgia, in any of the other centuries. It was Baltimore, in 1976. The time moved forward then, not backward. Nor did it circle round. The only time made sacred was the three days' deadline for payment imposed under force of law by the auctioneer. The news was not about ships reaching ports with fresh slave stock. It was about inflation, gasoline shortages. It was about oil-rich Arabs buying up the Sea Islands. It was about money and the lack of it and the fear of everything that made people afraid. I do not like to remember that time.

But while I am planning my trip, I remember the good things that I liked.

I liked Baltimore in summers and in winters. I liked the old harbor, the way it was before it was gentrified with shops and lights for the benefit of tourists. I liked to watch the boats and ships out on the water. I liked the old, worn bricks in certain streets, the ancient buildings, the squares with their statues, and the abundance of seafood from Chesapeake Bay. These aspects of Baltimore remind me of Savannah, where I grew up. There is a certain little square, I think on Monument Street in Baltimore, with a metal statue and cobblestones that reminds me of Pulaski Square in Savannah. When I lived in Baltimore, I liked to walk through the neighborhoods and watch people sitting on the steps of their narrow row houses to escape the summer heat. On hot summer mornings, in both cities, people wash down the steps of their houses and let them dry in the hot sunlight. The heat in both cities, because of their proximity to water, is humid and wet. People in Baltimore, like those in Savannah, accept sweat as an unfortunate incident of summer. In both cities, the early mornings and the early evenings are the best times for walking. People in both places are most polite during those cool and special times of the day.

The soul of Baltimore, for me, is the old Lexington Market on Lexington and Eutaw streets. It is a kind of warehouse off the downtown section that is crowded with little shops and concession stands, many of them selling crabcakes and other seafood. In this almost open-air market, all sections of Baltimore meet and breathe in common the moist aromas of fresh shrimp, oysters, crabs, every possible Atlantic Ocean fish, a variety of fruits, vegetables, and fresh meats. I remember oyster bars, where people stand and eat raw oysters after spicing them with condiments. I remember the refrigerated display cases featuring, among many other choices, row after row of uncooked crabcakes. These are a very special delicacy, made Maryland style. The basic recipe is a mixture of crabmeat (fresh lump, blue, backfin, or special) and eggs, bread crumbs, Worcestershire sauce, fresh parsley, mayonnaise, baking powder, salt, and a variety of spices. This mixture, after being caked in the bread crumbs, is deep-fat fried, drained, and served while moist and hot and brown. All crabcakes are good, but Maryland crabcakes have special ingredients, or spices, not found in those crabcakes made according to the recipes of other regions.

Unlike in Savannah, in Baltimore they have soft, white, wet, clinging snow during the winter months. It seldom gets cold enough for the snow to freeze, so it remains white and clear and fluffy in the bright winter sunlight. I liked that. I liked the way the white, sun-melting snow would slide lazily and waterily off the skeletal branches of high-reaching trees and plop wetly on anything beneath the boughs. In Savannah, during the winter months, we got only cold rain. Still, I did not mind walking in it, as long as I was warm and dry and walking very quickly. I consider the number eighty-six lucky for me. It was the number of my old newspaper route, my very first job, when I was a boy in Savannah. I used to walk that route six days a week, in the sweaty summer heat and in the cold winter rains, with my papers. I used to take a personal interest in the lives and health of all my customers along that route. I used to be sympathetic to their excuses for not having the money to pay their paper bills. I tried my best to have compassion for them. I believed, then, that everything would eventually even out.

I have always considered eighty-six my lucky number.

The Natural Facts of Death and Life in Baltimore, November 1993

I FLY FROM Iowa into New York, then rent a car at the Newark airport, in order to avoid the traffic of the city, and drive south on Interstate 95. It is late fall in the East, and all the bright, crisp, red and brown and green and gold colors have bled from the sparse stretches of trees lining the interstate. The last brown leaves are wilting and falling in the warm morning breezes, and the cars around me seem to be navigating at unnatural speeds, all heading homeward from the sadness of the fall. Then I realize that the pace of eastern interstate traffic is too fast for my driving skills, which have become settled now into the slow and easy habits of country roads. Neither do I have, any longer, personal investments in the landscape. I can no longer remember, or care about, where I was going to, or where I was returning from, when I parked at the official rest stops in New Jersey, Pennsylvania, Delaware, on my way up and down this road. My polarities have now become strictly east and west.

I am told, when I arrive at the office, that my own agent, Ms. Gayle Wilson, has been detained. While I wait for her, I listen to an elderly, extremely muscular black man who is flirting with the young receptionist at her desk. He has just retired, and is now about to close on a house, his first in a lifetime of working. He talks about the kindness of the Jewish woman who has sold it to him. He brags about the new appliances he has purchased. I think, while I listen to him talk, *This is what our struggle has been about all along.* That man, this late in his life, has become renewed by the ethic that exists in ownership. This has always been the certified way people show that they have moved up in life. It is what the society offers, and it is enough for most people. *What did I have against it all these years?* The man is joyous, flirting with the young black woman. He is no longer a laborer. He is now an owner. He is now her equal. He now has a house, new appliances, and is on the lookout for a companion who would want to share the castle of his dreams. *It has always been as simple as that.* I have not observed the styles of black people in many years. The kindly flirtation between the two of them reminds me of something familiar that I have almost forgotten. It seems to be something about language being secondary to the way it is used. The forgotten thing is about the nuances of sounds that only employ words as ballast for the flight of pitch and intonation. It is the pitch and the intonation that carry *meaning*. I had forgotten this.

Ms. Gayle Wilson, my agent, comes into the office. She is a very tall, very attractive black woman in formal dress. "I've just come from a funeral at my church," she tells me. "It was a close friend who died and I was an usher." We sit down and get to business. She hands me her brochure. It says she is active in the affairs of her church, her community, and in the organizations related to her business. She tells me, "I know of someone who is buying up houses out in that area. We can probably make a sale today. I'll call him up right now." She picks up her telephone, dials a number, and the ringing is answered immediately. She says, "Mr. Lee, I told you about that house coming up for sale out on Barclay? The owner is in my office right now. Good. Can you meet us over there in half an hour? Fine." She hangs up and says to me, "I think Mr. Lee will buy the house from you right away. He's a speculator. He buys up old houses and then fixes them for resale. He said he would meet us over there in half an hour."

She leaves the office to tell the receptionist where we will be.

A car crash calls my attention to the busy street outside the plateglass window of Ms. Wilson's office. Other people, including Ms. Wilson, rush out the front door. A speeding car has sideswiped another car, and this car has been knocked off the street, across the sidewalk and the narrow lawn, and into the brown wooden fence surrounding the real estate office. The driver's side of the car has caved in. The windshield glass is broken, cracked into white webs. Some men, white passersby and store clerks, are trying to ease the passenger out of the collapsed car. The passenger is an elderly woman, white, who seems to be in a daze. She wobbles like a rubber doll as they handle her. Her thin, vanilla-white hair is scattered on her head. I cannot see any blood. But the car seems totaled.

It is only an accident on the busy suburban street. But I watch the men crowd around the old woman. More and more of them come. There seems to be among them a desperate hunger to be helpful. The men, in their numbers, seem to be trying to make up for something. Although all their efforts are not needed, more and more men come from the service station across the street to push the car away from the wooden fence. There seems to be among them almost a lust for participation in some kindly, communal action.

Ms. Gayle Wilson comes back into her office.

I tell her that I think, now, that it would be inappropriate for her and Mr. Lee to meet me at the house. I say that first I must pay my respects to Mr. Butler.

Ms. Wilson agrees that this is the proper thing. She talks about the work she does in her church, about her love for rhyming poetry, about this afternoon's funeral, about the accident outside. We watch the crowd of men pushing the caved-in car away from the wooden fence, out of our view from the office window. The old woman has already been taken away. There has not been the sound

of a siren or the lights of an ambulance. I assume that the
crowd of men has grabbed this opportunity, too.

Ms. Wilson writes out detailed directions for my drive
back into the city and over to Barclay Street.

I promise to call her from Iowa in a few days.

Barclay is a right turn off Thirty-third Street, one block
before Greenmount. You are careful to not look at the
house on the corner you once rented. You drive straight
to 3114, two blocks to the right of Thirty-third, and park.
The street is making a resurgence. There is a new neighborhood store, and several of the houses have been refur-
bished and are up for sale. Careful sanding has restored
old blood to their red bricks. They seem freshly painted,
too, wailing confidently for occupants. This seems to you a
good sign. Life here is poised for movement, when spring
comes. But there is the same rusty, white-spotted swing
on the porch at 3114 Barclay. It is empty, speckled with
peeling paint, and seems ancient. You do not pause to look
at it. You knock, and a young black man opens the door.
He invites you into the overwarm living room. Mr. Butler
sits in his usual place: to the right of the door, in his old
armchair, against the window. He wears his gray touring
cap. He looks tired and old. His voice is only a croak. You
shake his hand but do not hold his hand, or look long at
him. Mr. Butler says to the young man, "This is the landlord. He came here from Iowa." The young man, who has
resumed his place on the sofa, answers, "Yes, sir." He is
sitting in Mrs. Washington's place at the right end of the
sofa, almost side by side with Mr. Butler. The television is

turned to a late afternoon game show. The room is over-warm and dusty, but still retains a feeling that is familiar.

The young man's name is Eric. He seems to be about sixteen or seventeen.

You express your sympathies to Mr. Butler and to Eric. Eric keeps nodding and saying to you "Yes, sir." You do not want this formality. You miss Mrs. Washington's otherworldly good cheer. You miss her smile. You miss her saying "The landlord come. Yes *indeed!* He come all the way from *Ioway!* Thank the Good Lord. Yes, yes in*deed!*" But her voice does not come except in memory. Eric says, "My daddy left my mama when I was born. My mama is Elizabeth McIntosh, my Aunt Channie's niece. Aunt Channie raised me while my mama worked. She was mama, daddy, aunt, uncle, parents, and grandparents to me. Yes, sir. I miss her. I come over here every evening and sit with Mr. Herbert. I don't know how he lives, sir, now that my Aunt Channie is gone."

You ask Eric if you can inspect the house. Eric asks Mr. Butler for his permission. The old man nods from his chair. Eric leads the tour. The small box of a basement contains only an old refrigerator and the ancient, red-rusted furnace. It is the old friend you have been nursing over all these years. It is so old it embarrasses you. "Why did she never mention the true condition of the furnace?" you ask Eric. He says, "My Aunt Channie didn't like to throw away nothing that could be fixed, sir. And she never liked to bother nobody. I gave her that refrigerator over there myself, because her old one was so bad." He leads you back up the loose, sagging basement steps to the dining room, where he shows you the cot where Mr. Butler sleeps. He is much too weak, Eric says, to climb the steps to the second floor. Eric leads the way up them. The top floor has three bedrooms and a bath. One of the bedrooms is obviously used by an occasional boarder. Another, Eric tells you, remains empty and ready as a place for guests. For an instant, this seems to you a very extravagant gesture for a person in poverty. Then you recollect the dusty picture of Jesus, about to knock, on the wall above the television. Here you almost laugh. Eric opens, and closes very quickly, the door to Mrs. Washington's bedroom. In the brief illumination of light, you can see her bed, made up, with its pillow in place, waiting. All of the ceilings in the rooms upstairs are cracked and peeling. You ask Eric why she never asked for repairs. He says, again, that she did not like to bother anybody with her problems. He says "sir" once more. The two of you go downstairs again, through the kitchen, and out onto the back porch. Its boards are broken and split. The wood is soft from age and weather. Eric says that Mr. Butler fell recently here. The twisted old tree still bends over the porch at an ugly angle, as if poised to grow confidently through the broken wooden porch and into the house. The bent tree, with its roots encased in concrete, seems to be nature's revenge on the illusory order of city life. You suddenly say to Eric, "Please don't keep calling me sir." He says, "But I *always* say sir to older people."

This also reminds you of something old.

Elizabeth McIntosh, Eric's mother, comes into the house then. Mrs. Washington was her mother's sister, she tells you. She talks freely about her Aunt Channie's life. Mrs. Washington had been married once, but had no children. She had come to Baltimore from a rural community in South Carolina. She had worked as a short-order cook in several restaurants around the city, until bad health caused her to retire. She was, of course, a churchwoman. "She loved you," Elizabeth says. "She considered you part of the family. She always wrote a letter to you to send with the rent check. Even when she was sick in bed, she insisted on dictating the letters to me. She kept saying, 'You *have* to write it. I *always* send a letter with my check.'"

You ask Elizabeth to send you, in Iowa, a copy of Mrs. Washington's funeral program.

You tell Mr. Butler, watching from his armchair, that everything will be fine.

You call Eric back to the back porch and tell him that the needed repairs will be made.

Eric says, "Yes, sir."

When you go back into the living room, you sit in Mrs. Washington's place on the sofa, before Eric can get to it. You sit there. You look at the game show on the television, and at the picture on the wall behind it. You ask Elizabeth whether Mrs. Washington ever prayed.

"Almost every hour of every day," Elizabeth answers.

You still sit there. You watch a few minutes of television with Mr. Butler. Then, for some reason, you ask the three of them to pray for you.

Then you want to see again, as quickly as possible, the brown stubble left, after fall harvest, in the rolling, open fields of Iowa.

But you still drive around the area until the streets begin to connect again in your memory. You are trying hard now to remember the other things you still have to do. You will have to find a short way back to the interstate, heading north. While driving, you look for your favorite bookstore on Greenmount. It is gone. So is the movie theater that was once several doors away. So is the Chinese restaurant. But the Ennoch Pratt Library branch on Thirty-third and Barclay is still there. You decide that you do not have time to drive past the stadium. You will have to hurry, to better negotiate the early evening traffic collecting near Interstate 95, heading north. But you do stop, impulsively, at the liquor store on Greenmount, not for any purchase but just to see another familiar place. Old memories are returning now. But the yelling Jewish owners are gone. The new owners seem to be Koreans. Black clerks still do the busywork.

Now the connection you have been waiting for is suddenly made. You can now remember the route from here to the Lexington Market. You can remember the names of streets from here to there. Your plan now is to get some crabcakes and find some way to keep them fresh enough to survive the trip back to Iowa. You will need ice and a plastic cooler. And you will need luck in shipping the plastic cooler on two different flights. There is an element of madness in this plan, but it also contains a certain boldness that you have not felt in many years. You determine to do it.

To get to the Lexington Market from Greenmount Avenue, you must turn left onto Thirty-third Street and head south. At the point where Thirty-third intersects

St. Paul, you should take another left. The buildings and campuslands of Johns Hopkins should be in the distance as you turn left onto St. Paul. You should follow St. Paul Street south all the way downtown, pass the more stately row houses on both left and right, pass the shops and bars and restaurants near North Avenue, the mostly black section of St. Paul, pass Penn Station, and go all the way to the traffic circle on Monument Street, the old street with cobblestones and a bronze statue of Washington at the center of the circle, like those they have in the squares in Savannah. The other landmark here is the Walters Gallery. You should pass Monument Street and keep going down St. Paul. You are now approaching the downtown section of Baltimore. Here the buildings become taller and newer. The traffic becomes much more concentrated and the people walk with much greater purpose. On your left, just off the corner of Charles Street, should be the old building where your painter friend has a loft. Just beyond Charles, the buildings become mostly commercial. The lights of the harbor should be invisible in the distance, farther down St. Paul. On Franklin Street, you should take a right. Several blocks down, the main branch of the Ennoch Pratt Library should appear on your left. Go several blocks beyond the Ennoch Pratt, then turn left onto Eutaw. This is near the street of the Lexington Market. Find parking wherever you can.

The Threat of Downsizing at the Soul of the City

WE FIND THAT the market has not changed that much after all these years. There are now some upscale boutiques and displays, and Korean families now run some of the produce stands and shops. But the old oyster bars are still there, as are the high, narrow tables where people add condiments to their oysters and stand while eating them raw. We breathe in the same familiar smells of fresh fish, flowers, fruits, vegetables, and raw meats. We see the same familiar mixture of people from all segments of the city, blending one accord of accents into the commercial mass.

All of the seafood stands display crabcakes. Rather than waste time, we decide on those displayed in the showcase of just one stand. The most appealing, and the most expensive, are the lump crabcakes, made up in round, crumb-coated balls. They swell up out of their trays like overfed bellies. The other crabcakes on display—backfin, special, regular— are less expensive and therefore less attractive. The black woman standing beside us is also deciding. She is partial to the lumps. "Them's the best ones," she says. "They taste best just out the pan. But all these other crabcakes is just as good." We decide on two lump crabcakes, to be eaten now, and a dozen regulars packed in ice to go.

Behind the counter of the stand, three black teenage boys in white aprons and white paper hats are filling orders. Behind them, at the stove, an elderly black woman lowers and raises webbed metal trays of crabcakes and French fries into deep frying pits of hot bubbling oil. Around the counter people lean, as if at communion, waiting for their hot orders to come. The woman and the boys seem to us essential to the operation. They set the standard of taste. The owner, or the manager, a white man, hovers near the cash register, giving orders in an unfamiliar accent. Then we remember that this is Baltimore, where the musical pitch of the South meets and smothers the gruffness of Germanic habits.

We are savvy enough to say that we are a tourist from out in Iowa, have heard good things about Maryland crab-cakes, and want to take a dozen of them back home. We will need a dozen of the regulars, uncooked and packed in ice, to go, and two of the lump, cooked to eat now. The boy who takes our order communicates the problem to the owner. He comes up to the counter and says, "There ain't no way you can keep them fresh, even in ice, if you're drivin' such a distance." We respond that we are flying out of New York tomorrow afternoon, and that only enough ice is needed to keep the crabcakes fresh long enough, this evening, to drive into New York. There they can be frozen in the apartment of a friend. From New York, tomorrow, it will only be a four-hour flight to Iowa. Much like the mail. As an incentive, we add that people in Iowa seldom taste fresh Maryland crabcakes and that a desire to share a delicacy is at the basis of this gift. But in order to remain a gift, we say, it is essential that the crabcakes keep moving. If they lose refrigeration before New York, they will have to be eaten there. They will then become a simple meal. But if they should survive the trip into the city, and are frozen quickly, and then, tomorrow, survive again the two separate flights into Iowa—if the gift keeps moving at the same speed as it thaws—then, with luck, it can be shared with friends in Iowa tomorrow evening. Our plan, we say, is to ensure that some good part of Maryland will take up residence in the memories of friends in Iowa. We say again: It is essential that the gift keep moving. If it stops moving at any point before it can be given, the crabcakes will thaw quickly and lose the basic intention of their identity. They *must*, therefore, be shared with Iowa friends to remain essentially what they are. But to ensure this, they must be kept moving. Once they stop moving, short of their goal, they will become just another meal. The action of the original intention will have then been defeated. To avoid this fate for them, we *must* have lots of ice. Fresh ice, if it is needed, might be found along the interstate heading back to Newark. We want now to risk this chance.

The manager becomes suspicious that we are mad. But we also sense that it is his bottom-line business to sell. Our request, or our outlandish demand, upsets the Teutonic order of his scale of values. To him, and to his black workers, the calculation of air time is as distant from the imagination as the lonely status of the "I" in uppercase. Perhaps he sees unrelenting cornfields in his imagination, or a bleak world of perpetual pork. Perhaps it is this that arouses his sympathy, and his skills. He gives orders to the black boy waiting at the counter. The boy nods politely but cautiously while he listens, his slow-moving eyes seeing the details of a radical plan. We enlist him deeper into our designs by ordering two lump crabcakes, deep-fat fried, to be eaten now, while we wait. This is the familiar thing. He passes the order to the black woman, the short-order cook, frying at the stove.

We are satisfied now that something that can be shown will be brought back from Baltimore into Iowa. We have been, and *are,* of both places. The balance between them that was disrupted has now been temporarily restored. But, while waiting, we become bothered by our lack of decisiveness, by the steady weakening of our initial strong resolve. A muscular "I" in the uppercase drove into Baltimore, but a fragmented self, crowded now into the lowercase, will be driving out. We worry over this problem when our steaming crabcakes come and we eat them at the counter. They are delicious. This is the body and blood that had been lost. This is the content of the cup that was long quested for. *It restoreth our soul.* We eat them, though, without the ketchup from the counter. The red would only spoil the delicate browns of their color. We savor what is already there in them. The taste and texture and wetness take us back many years, back to our original appetite for crabcakes. *This* is the body. *This* is the blood. "I bring you news of one who died and has returned. If winter comes, can spring be far behind?"

We think that this is the hidden basis of all belief.

But as we now consume the remaining crabcake, the missing part of us begins to reclaim its old, accustomed place. It says to us we have become sentimental about Mrs. Washington and her scant facts. She died. We had carried her above and beyond all expectation before she died. We have taken losses. We are reminded, now, that we should follow through on our original plan to sell the house immediately. Earlier today, we recollect, we almost became responsible again for its taxes and repairs. The two hundred dollars each month that will come now from Mr. Butler will barely cover the taxes. We should have come *here first,* to the Lexington Market, to satisfy our renewed appetite for Maryland crabcakes. We have done that now, even though in the wrong order of visits. But we can take comfort in the fact that Ms. Gayle Wilson, the real estate agent, is still available. She will maintain the business sense we need to rely on now. Our house can still be sold. Repairs will only enhance its value on the market, we are reminded. In the end, the house will have much more curbside appeal. It has never before had this, except during impersonal auctions. We are remembering now that it has been sentimentality, and that alone, that has undermined our purpose. The entire day has been a series of impersonal assaults on the muscularity of our self-standing "I." *I resent this.* It has taken us many, many years to move upward from the lowercase, and it has taken only one day for our *I* to be undermined into a wilderness of scattered, self-defeating selves. We sense that Eric has had something to do with this development, *I* should not have allowed him to continue saying *"Yes, sir. Yes, sir."* His subtle plea implied elderliness, and therefore liens of loyalty. We recollect now that these were snares, set to pull us down into the confusions of the lowercase. We recollect Eric's voice now, with no hint of a muscular "I" in it, chanting its leveling litany: *My Aunt Channie was like daddy, mama, grandmother, grandfather, aunt, and uncle to me.* *"Yes, sir. Yes, sir."* Now that *my Aunt Channie is dead, I come over every evening and sit with Mr. Herbert.* Eric has an "I" that is employed for only limited purposes. It would not know what to do if it became dislodged from the clutch of fealty. We follow this thread, and re-collect into it the new language in Mrs. Washington's last letter. *Dear James Family.* Another subtle assault against the self-standing of our uppercase. Even Mr. Butler had been uncomfortable in claiming the autonomy of personal loss for himself. He generalized his pain. Those were the traps, we are reminded now, that pulled our purposeful "I" down into the lowercase. This is why we are now who we are *now.* This is the source of our present mood of indecision. We decide, now finished with our crabcakes, that the only solution is to say the final goodbye that was originally intended.

Our dozen regular crabcakes are ready. The manager puts them proudly on display. They have been wrapped lightly in foil. The foil package has been wrapped inside layers of plastic bags. There is a layer of ice in each plastic bag. There are three plastic bags, each containing a layer of crushed ice, cooling the crabcakes. We pay our bill. The owner says, "Now we ain't go'n guarantee the ice will last till New York. But we done our best to get you there." Then he whispers to the black boy who is making change. The young man goes away, then returns with a large soft drink, ice cold, in a plastic cup. "One for the road. A gift," the manager says. Both of them take a mysterious pleasure in offering the liquid to us.

It is the impulse beneath the boosterism that contains the mystery.

Our drive to Interstate 95, heading north, is easier from the Lexington Market area. We drive much more comfortably now, inside the flow of early evening traffic. We plan ahead to the bus from Newark into the city, and the short cab ride from Port Authority to the friend's apartment on Riverside Drive. This friend is Japanese, and we think we should offer some of the crabcakes as a gift. The crabcakes will be cool by then, and a few might benefit from the changed intention. They might reach a much more healthy end as a commodity, or as a souvenir brought back from travel. The Japanese are great lovers of souvenirs. The presentation of one is considered a prologue to each meeting. It is not the quality of the gift, they say, but the purity of the intention behind it that is considered sacred. But then the apostate "I" of the scattered self reminds us that we are still stuck in lowercase, moving now from one small village-sense into another. We had thought *they* would be left behind us now, in the city. But even here, speeding purposefully through the evening traffic of Walt Whitman's south New Jersey, we find ourselves still de-selfing. We are still stuck in the village mode of mind.

We pull ourselves into full registration and *vote* with unanimity.

It is determined, once again, that our plan should remain the original one. All twelve crabcakes will be left overnight in the friend's freezer. After ten or so hours there, they should be frozen solid. By tomorrow afternoon, when we begin our flight, the crabcakes should still be fresh. They will fly next to us on the airplane, like express-mailed letters. All baggage will arrive together, *re-collected,* from the separation caused by the two flights. When the brown, harvested cornfields are seen, we will know that we are *home.* All of us, the friends included, will have a feast. Once the gift is put into motion again, around the dinner table, the lure of de-selfing will have abated, and the other parts of us that have been scattered can be reclaimed.

Our "I" will be al home again, and can make its best decisions unfettered by the chains of ancient memories, is the thought that is kept fixed as we drive north.

But once at home again, beyond the welcome of the brown, harvested Iowa cornfields, there is a sudden decision to refreeze the crabcakes.

The Rescue of a Self from the Snares of the Past

THERE IS HARD work involved in relocating a respectable batch of the letters. They must be looked for in boxes of old letters, papers, magazines, bills that have been stored over the years in various corners of the basement. They must be put into a pile on the dining room table and reread. It is here that an initial intuition proves to be the correct one. The letters report few facts. They never vary in their language and in their focus. Nor do they ever mention the rent checks that accompany them. I find enough of the letters to pinpoint the dates of several repairs on the old furnace, one replacement of electric wiring, one occasion of work on leaking water pipes. These have been the only emergencies. The costs of the smaller repairs are always deducted from the rent. The receipts are always enclosed. These occasions are the only ones for news about reality. All other letters say almost the same ritual things: "Everything is fine," "God bless you and the family," "Thank the Good Lord," "By By." I realize now how accustomed *I* have become to these monthly reports on the nonfacts of life. Still, over the years they have become a respite of some kind. They have been monthly reminders of the insubstantial elements comprising even the most permanent of things.

But as I continue reading through the letters, my mature instincts keep reminding me that no human being is this simple. No human being could be *only* the repetition of the same old assertions from one month to the next. I do not expect a secret life in Mrs. Washington, but I find myself needing something more to mourn. It may be that the years have taught me to be untrusting of what once seemed simple, uncomplicated, pure. My mind has grown used to being vigilant. I have learned that things that seem to be *are not* what they seem to be. The thing that seems most like itself has, most likely, been calculated to seem to be that way. There is always something hidden. There is always that extra fact. I continue reading through the letters, all that I can find, for the clue that will lead to the private intuition, which in turn, in time, will merge with a larger and expanding reality, and give rise to the experience of truth. This is the metaphysic of detectives during times of universalized corruption. It is also the refuge of cynics. I cannot truly move against Mr. Butler until the self-interested action can be rationalized in terms of some hidden fact. This is, after all, the way of the world. It is the art of self-interested, savage discovery.

The funeral program, sent from Baltimore by Elizabeth McIntosh, arrives at my home a week after me. I let the letter sit unopened for several days before reviewing the folded sheet. It is called a Homegoing Service for Channie Washington. A faded picture of her is below this title. She looks the way I first saw her on the porch. She looks dressed for church on Sunday morning. Her funeral had taken place on October 26, at the Second Antioch Baptist Church, 3123 Barclay Street, in Baltimore. Her church, like her family, was only a few doors away. The obituary recites the basic facts of her life.

Channie Washington, daughter of the late Cornelius and Annie Gibson, was born on January 29, 1915, in Hartsville, South Carolina. She departed this life on October 21, 1993, after a brief illness.

She received her education in the Darlington County Public Schools, in South Carolina.

Channie was married to the late Isaac Washington.

At a young age, she moved to Baltimore, Maryland.

Later, she became a member of the Second Antioch Baptist Church. She served faithfully as a Missionary.

She worked at several restaurants, as a Short Order Cook, until she retired.

She loved to cook and enjoyed having her family and friends on Sundays, for her big meals.

Channie was a loveable and well-liked person. She loved her family and could never say no to anyone in need. She will be greatly missed.

She leaves to cherish her memory: her long-time beloved companion, Herbert Butler; two sisters, Mrs. Olivia Allen and Mrs. Rebecca Hankins of Norfolk, Virginia; eleven nieces; twelve nephews; fifteen great nieces; sixteen great nephews; fifteen great great nieces and nephews; and a host of other relatives and friends.

> God saw the road was getting rough
>   The hills were hard to climb;
> He gently closed her loving eyes
>   And whispered, "Peace Be Thine."
> Her weary nights are passed
> Her ever patient, worn out frame
>   Has found sweet rest at last.
>   Humbly Submitted,
>   The Family

The opening hymn was "What a Friend We Have in Jesus."

There were remarks, a solo, a reading of the obituary, by the various sisters and brothers of Mrs. Washington's church.

It comes to me now that Mrs. Washington had never been alone on that porch when I first saw her. For all her life, she had been an intimate part of something much larger than herself. She had not really needed my help. My old friend, the teacher, had been right all along. I might have passed by the scene, and nothing tragic would have happened to her. She might have been allowed by the new owner to remain in the house. She might have moved in with one of her two sisters, or with one of her many nieces or nephews. Her church might have found another place for her. The welfare people, if all else had failed, might have moved both her and Mr. Butler into a state-supported retirement home, where their lives might have been much more protected and pleasant during these last eighteen years. My old mentor had been right all along. I had taken upon myself, in a publicly arrogant way, a responsibility that was not my own. Now the needed fact begins to emerge in outline.

I had grown drunk on an infatuation with my own sense of "goodness" and had employed Mrs. Washington, and also Mr. Butler, as a prop for the background of the self-display I had wanted, then, to dramatize. I had challenged the white men in the crowd, inspired by motives I had rationalized into a higher sense of things, when I had, all along, been an actual member of the crowd. "Father, I am not like these other men. I pray ten times a day, I give tithes in the synagogue, I minister to widows and orphans, I . . ."

The fact comes clearly to me then: a value is not a value as long as it depends for its existence on a comparison with something else.

Then I remember a something else. It is a something else recollected from a time much longer ago than Baltimore. This memory merges with Mr. Herbert Butler and Elizabeth McIntosh and with the young man named Eric. He was just a baby, two or three porches away on Barclay Street, when I first bought the house. I think to myself, What if she had been forced to move away and had not been available to Eric during those years, after his father abandoned him and his mother went to work? How different would Eric's life be now if Mrs. Washington had not been there?

I think about this additional fact.

I think, again, that time *must* be a cycle, because this fact brings me back, back, back to my *self.*

I *re-collect* what there was in Eric that had made me so uncomfortable.

Now I remember. Now I remember it all.

Eric Abstracted and Recombined

WHEN RUNNING AWAY, you always found that first pit stop. Your plans have been fueled by fear, by aloneness, by questions the answers to which no one seems to know because no one is *really* there. You are far past fantasy now, young adolescent, pushing with passion against all that does not push back. Nothing does. No one is there who

has time to care. You are feeling the freedom to test yourself against something larger than yourself, something
familiar at first, something gentle that will still push
back. This becomes the place of the pit stop in your plans
for running away. You always go there first, to the envi-
rons of the familiar, to gather strength for this first solo
flight out into the world. This familiar foreign place is
always on the outskirts of this woman's voice. She is a few
doors down the block, a few blocks distant, the other side
of town. Her house is a safe place to stop during the first
part of your flight. She stands over you, looking down.
She says things like "Come in, boy. Take a load off your
mind." She says, "Come on in and rest your feels." The
renegotiation usually began in this ritual way. She is too
old to be a bitch and much too far removed from this
world to be a ho'. She is not the mammy of folklore. In
the distant past of her life she has made the same mistakes you are inviting. You are not "black male" to her,
but blood. She cares about the special ways it flows. She
knew your father before he was your father, and your
mother before the girlish dreams in her died. It is not her
fault they have been taken from you by life. Unlike you,
she long ago learned to expect not much good from it.
She knows that you must learn to do the same. Her life
has been a preparation for the worst, and her small joys
derive from anything less. It is life's hard lesson, this special peace that is past all understanding, and she will take
her time in teaching it. But just now she protects you
from the central mystery she has learned to master. She
does not yet want to instruct in the quiet joy she has lo-

cated on the ebb of unrelieving pain. This will be life's lesson, not her own. She cooks. She seems always to be at home. Her place is where you pause to get your bearings for the road. Her familiar name, the name you call her, always has two sounds, preceded by "Aunt." They represent her as solid and without pretension. "Chi-na." "Beulah." "Gus-sie." "Ma-ry." *"Chan-nie."* She is the eternal aunt of archetype, not the mammy. Hers is the first outside model of finished woman you explore. She has lost all belief in even the most pedestrian possibilities of the self-standing "I" and has learned to live carefully inside a populated "we." She is the fountainhead, the base at the whisk of the broom that keeps the "we," the "us," collected. You are one of the straws about to stray. You feel safe running away as far as her house, for a pause at this pit stop, because you know there is fellow feeling kept in unlimited supply for you there. But she still makes you feel uncomfortable. She has no material proof for her belief in God, but believes anyway. This increases her mystery. She has learned to see miracles in small, comic things: it is not too hot or too cold, a cool breeze comes through the window, the old furnace still operates all through winter. She also irritates you by giving all credit to "The Man Upstairs," to "The Good Lord," even when she can clearly see the causal physics involved. You want to teach her what you are learning in the streets, from radio, from television. But you also take secret comfort in the fact that her higher world, the one above your frustrations in this one, is viewed by her as under the strict control of a good *Man*. You would not want to be as burdened as *He* is, but at the same time you are glad that He is there. He is the only Man, as far as you can see, to whom she defers. She talks always of His will. Because she is on such intimate terms with Him, you never consider that this man is white, or female. Her manner assures you that the world where He lives is beyond all such concerns. This man has to do only with things that are ultimate. He lists lies. He watches sparrows. He knows all secrets. There are no private plans that will not come to light. This man already knows why you are running. While she talks and looks at you, you begin to believe that she knows, too. Coming here always seems to cause a reconstruction. Maybe today, after all, you will not leave the comfort of her house. But tomorrow, or the next time, you will not come here first. You will just continue down the road. When she sees you again, years from now, you will be worldly, a grown man, with all the things you worry about not having now. You will pay her back for the meal she is giving you. You will bring back solid, seeable proofs that The Man Upstairs is much too busy with the flights of sparrows to see into the hidden corners you have found. The proofs you will bring back will be from fairyland, from Jacksonville, from the New York she has never seen. They might come, much more quickly, from the crack house just several blocks away, where other boys your age are already making money. Boys much younger than yourself have already made their own miracle. They have abstracted the assembly line from McDonald's and sell, with a smart efficiency that you admire, small plastic bags of crack to white people from the suburbs who drive by.

One, some boy you know personally and admire, Bro' or Dupe or Home, takes the orders; one, farther on, collects money; and the third boy, at the end of the block, just by the corner, delivers the plastic sandwich bags, the very ones that used to hold your lunch at school, to the eager white hand reaching out the window of the car. You have been invited to become part of this process, to stand at one end of the McDonald's line or at the other. It looks easy. Sometimes, in your bed at night, in the quiet and the darkness, you can imagine such an assembly line stretching *down* southward from Savannah, into Jacksonville, Miami, Tampa, or *up* from Baltimore, north, like in the old stories, to Dover, Philly, Newark, New York, New Haven, Hartford, and Boston. *Phillymeyork*. With yourself at either end of the line, taking McDonald's orders or delivering white dust. *Phillymeyork. Cowboys and silver dollars*. Meanwhile, now, she is talking at the child who is leaving you, in a language that no longer fits the way things are. Maybe tomorrow, or sometime soon, you will be going all the way. But for now, with the food and considering the time of day . . . and considering her sparrows and the ever-watching eyes she apparently looks into, and sees through . . . *In later years,* close friends will tell you that in moments of frustration you tend to say *"Oh Lord!"* You will think back on the source of this, trying to remember. It is somehow connected, you recollect, with firm intentions that have come unglued. It will be connected with memories that are embarrassing. This Lord you petition will somehow have to do with the old dream of money, and with memories of fellow feeling and food, and also with the natural flow of sympathy. But you are a man now and no longer think much about childhood. Still, you will begin to *recollect* a tired black woman who stood in her doorway between the lures of the streets and you. She was one of your first loves. Inside her door you always felt a degree of safety, the sense of which has now been lost. But these recollections of dependency now threaten to intrude upon your present self-possession. You are self-made, in the terms of, and in the view of, the principalities and powers of *this* world. You know no other Lord beyond yourself. Besides, you say to those who heard your voice reaching, it would be crazy to call into the empty air for help. The voice that was heard was not your own. It possibly slipped out from the locked travel trunks of another time. It was a simple error in articulation . . . *But for now, here inside this house, in this be-foretime,* all appeals to the other world belong to her. You confess to her, while eating, your fear that the holes in your world cannot be fixed. You do not expect her to understand. She does not understand. But at the same time she is there, has always been there, just to listen. It is enough while she feeds you, while she talks in her private language. She cooks the things she likes best that you do not like. You eat them anyway. She talks, selectively, about her own early life, in her own Old Country. She tells stories about the old-fashioned time in the old-fashioned place. She says things like "Take the bitter with the sweet." She says things like "Catch more flies with honey than with vinegar." But her language does not enter into the sore spots of *your* problems. It is only a meaningless

counterthrust of words that obscures *your own specifics.*
She always finds ways to turn you away from yourself,
away from the life-and-death issues that first stalled you
at her door. You had come to her for just a hint of understanding. You wait long for this, but it never comes. You
eat the meal and decide to not come back again. But you
always do come back, each time you make fresh steps toward that better world beyond her door. Her home is the
secret pit stop you visit first, for food, for fuel, before continuing on up the road. You know that you could get
there much more quickly if she were not there. But she is
always there, like the police squad cars, like the ticket
agent in the toll booth at the entrance to the interstate,
who has already memorized the exact price of travel up or
down the road. She warns you to be careful and to watch
your speed. She inspires you to slow down. She becomes
the counterthrust to your full-forward. Sometimes she
seems to be the bitch your older friends have learned to
moan about. You think she will always be in your path, like
a stoplight frozen forever on blood red. But one day, quite
suddenly, she is not. You grieve some, but soon find the
loss is less important than the life ahead of you. She can be
forgotten. You still retain a mother and a growing lease on
life. At her funeral you take comfort in reciting, in line
with her beliefs, that the two of you will meet again. You
move on in your own life, not really remembering much,
until one day it happens. *You see her.* The armies of the
world have massed to remove her from her house. The
crowd does not know the importance of the place to her, *or
to you.* They see only something that is free-floating above

the ground, obsolete, old. They see a rundown row house. You see a temple. It is the place where she *must be* for those times when you run away. The crowd does not understand this house's history. It cannot contemplate that something larger is involved. *"My Aunt Chan-nie-Chi-na-Beu-lah-Gus-sie-Ma-ry* must *be there for me. "* Her house is your one refuge from the world. In that place your "I" is a less troubled "we." She has always lived a few doors down the street, a few blocks away, a rapid run across the backdirt lanes of town. You have grown used to dropping in and sitting. She has always been your rock of ages, who lifted you *up* above all undertows. You do not worry as long as she is there. But the crowd cannot see this always unfinished business. It threatens the unseeable self that has always lived between the two of you. It is cutting a connection that cannot be encased in reason. You cannot tell it that you have come to pause here and eat your meal before continuing down or up the road. Perhaps you can say that you *must* sit evenings with Mr. Herbert. Tell the crowd *anything* that will *make it go away . . .!*

I UNDERSTAND NOW why I claimed Eric's place on the sofa: the source of the bond we share was in that special seat.

I had sensed this *something,* almost eighteen years ago, during my walk that sweaty July morning.

After exploring up and down both coasts, *I* had circled back *home.*

~⟨⟨⟩⟩~

Now I search again for the *nonfacts* in Mrs. Washington's last letter, the one sent in September, with the meaning of its new language suddenly clarified.

"Dear James Family": She was drawing me closer in, *claiming.*

"Only a few lines to let you hear from us": *De-selfing.*

"I am doing much better now": *De-selfing.*

"Mr. Butler is fine": *Beloved.*

"Give the family our love": *Consideration, same monthly basis.*

"I will close my letter but not our love": *"My" ends, "Our" lives on. Offer.*

"May God Bless you all with much love and Happiness": *Source of future surplus, to back offer.*

"By By": *Extra understanding concealed in formulaic signature.*

"Channie Washington and Herbert": *Lifelong tenants.*

In the new ways I am now sensing beyond drinking thoughts, this last letter is Mrs. Channie Washington's last will and testament. I can read the nonfacts now. She has drawn me into her family. She has affirmed the stability of the present *status quo.* The declaration of her family's love stretching far into the future is her offer of consideration for something. It seems to be the kiting of the present circumstance against the surplus of some future time. There is a promise of abundant giving to balance something given of my own.

That is the way it has been for almost eighteen years.

NOW I READ back from the nonfacts and reconstruct the facts. Because she knew she was dying, Mrs. Washington was looking out for her family. She was intent on sheltering her beloved. She was deeply skilled in the uses of the intimate nonlanguage of black people, the language that only employed words as ballast and sound. Because the money rent she paid had never been sufficient, she had grown used to sending what compensation she could. Now she was offering, from the surplus she expected, the same rate of extra compensation far into the future. Mrs. Washington was stationed in future time, looking back on the now, making her usual spiritual adjustment in her monthly rent.

This nonlanguage was her offer to lock me in, as the landlord of her home, at the usual rate of payment, for many years to come. Mrs. Washington was offering a renewal of our old spiritual contract, locating future rent adjustments in the only source of surplus she knew. She had touched the most ultimate expression of kiting.

There was no will in the world sufficient to compete with the power of this offer. Mrs. Washington had always *known better.*

IT IS ONLY now that I unfreeze my crabcakes and begin to eat them. Now I do not worry about their freshness, or about how they taste. Now they represent only a secret signature, the symbolic acceptance of an offer.

Disneyland

NOT LONG AGO, as a kind of joke, I sent Rachel, my daughter, by E-mail, a line from an old song by Lambert, Hendricks, and Ross and Louis Armstrong:

> If you're king for only a day,
> How'd you go about having your way . . .?

This is the answer that came back:

If I were king, people couldn't blast their bass players in their cars, and if they did they would be punished by listening to "All Things Considered" on NPR all day long. Except that (if I were king) NPR wouldn't have much to report on the radio. Only good news. And so they would fill up the airtime by playing songs backwards and giving $100 to listeners who can name the tune. Everyone would have to smile at least once a day! Band-Aids wouldn't hurt when you yanked them off sores; the walls in dentists' offices would be covered with Waterhouse and Rosetti murals instead of lame, symmetrical, diamond patterns; and no one would have to listen to elevator music while on hold—only Swing. If I were king oranges would grow prepeeled, and pens wouldn't leak, and no one would be named Gertrude. Parks would have giant tree houses with signs that read: People of Any Height May Climb! Anyone could order off a damn kiddy menu, and swivel chairs would be a requirement for every dinner table—so if conversation got really boring people could twirl around instead. Everyone would have their own ideas about religion and no judgments about anyone else's. . . . [Weddings:] At twilight everyone would wander around a giant park with spouting fountains and a double rainbow would streak the sky. A church chime would ring at 7:00 p.m. (you know, the one that sounds like our doorbell) and that would be the sign for everybody to make a circle (not caring or even wondering if you're standing next to a bum, a Ph.D., or a movie star) and do the hokeypokey. That's what it's all about.

I was amazed by the reach and vitality of Rachel's imagination as she attempted to reorder the world according to her own sense of happiness. I sent her another E-mail:

You have learned that God created the world in six days, and on the seventh day He rested. But this is not entirely true. I have heard it said that on the seventh day God was not yet pleased with His creations. So on that day He created another thing that would be able to celebrate all the work He had done on the first six days. On the seventh day God created IMAGINA-TION, and he gave this thing dominion over all else He had created. The person who is blessed with this is able to stand in his own place and at the same time project himself into another person's place, see from the eyes of that person, and understand the world from that person's point of view. This gift is called "compassion," and it is a very, very rare thing.

Rachel, at eighteen, is doubly privileged. She has had imaginative as well as emotional support, all that I could give her from a great distance, for all her life. She seems to be a very happy and self-directed young woman. She graduated from high school in Charlottesville, Virginia, on June 5, 1997. She came to Iowa City for ten days, and then went off to New York to enroll in the Alvin Ailey Summer Dance Workshop. I supported her eight weeks in New York as a kind of graduation gift to her. Other friends in New York—Nancy Ramsey, Stanley Crouch, Albert Murray and his family, Faith Childs, Suketu and Sunita Mehta, Ana Debevoise, Sherman Malone—supported her emotionally. Rachel has benefited from being "closely held" by impromptu structures of dependability, which can be improvised around friends in any other part of the United States, as well as in England, Japan, and Australia. Both her life and my own have been blessed

by instances of kindly interference which, while renewing our spirits, have taught me that the increase in the
range of their possibility depends on one's involvement in
the lives of people outside of one's own group. This is the
Great Road that Rachel and I have traveled since she was
a baby. Now that she is eighteen, and enrolled in college, I
think and hope, and even pray, that she is secure and well
adjusted and whole in the deepest human sense.

In a recent correspondence with a divorced writer, he
expressed how extremely painful his isolation from his
daughter was. He loved her a great deal; she lived with her
mother in Atlanta, while he lived in Baltimore. In writing
back to him about this modern condition of alienation
between fathers and children, an alienation that results
from divorce, I restrained an impulse to quote to him a
line from a song in Walt Disney's *Peter Pan*: "You can fly,
you can fly, you can fly."

I know the truth of this from my own experience.

I will not give in to the temptation to finger all the details of my own divorce except to say that it was extremely
complicated and extremely bitter. All my efforts to negotiate a peaceful end to a very bad marriage failed, and
this void was quickly filled by predatory lawyers. Since
I had announced publicly that my only goal was to get
appropriate time with my daughter and then get out of
Charlottesville, Rachel, who was then not quite two years
old, became a pawn in the manipulation of lawyers and
other, hidden forces that were determined that I would
remain "captive." She was withheld from me through a
series of devices, even when visitation times had already

been scheduled. When I responded in anger, my voice was recorded and used against me at another time. But it was here that an instance of what I have called "kindly interference" took place. I went to see Shirley Porter, a black woman who worked as a nanny for mothers in the Charlottesville community. Shirley was a wise and kindly woman, one who wanted to be fair. Since Rachel spent most of her nights at Shirley's home, while being withheld from me, I would go to Shirley's home in the early evenings, eat dinner with her and Rachel, and help Shirley give Rachel a bath. Then I would sleep on the floor next to Rachel's crib. The next morning, before the other "mommies" brought their children to Shirley's house, I would help Shirley give Rachel breakfast, and even share the meal with her. If any of the "mommies" showed up early, while I was still there, I would hide in Shirley's closet until they left. On those Sundays when Rachel was with me, I would take her to Shirley's church. The two of us would sit, Rachel between us, on the same bench. Shirley Porter risked her own economic well-being to help us in this way.

In the early spring of the following year, 1981, a second small miracle occurred. I had been trying my best to heed the advice of friends in other parts of the country: "*Get out of there!*" I saw two jobs being advertised—one at Tucson, by Vance Bourjaily, and another at Iowa, by Jack Leggett. Both men were understanding, but Jack Leggett was especially kind. On a Sunday morning, about one month later, he called me in Charlottesville and said, "Jim, the job is yours in the fall, if you are able to take it. In addition, we want you to teach summer school." Jack had a gentle laugh, an easy, patrician manner. I believe that he was incapable of kicking anyone who was down. It was simply a matter of breeding and habit.

But the most important incident of kindly interference, the one that set Rachel and me on the pathway leading to the Great Road, came in May of that same year. By this time I had secured, through the legal system, some visitation time with Rachel. We had one overnight every other weekend, plus one afternoon together on Wednesdays. One Saturday evening when I brought Rachel to my small apartment, I saw an Express Mail envelope taped to the door. I tore it down, believing it was another notice from one of the credit card companies to which, back then, I owed my future. Rachel and I had worked out certain rituals for her overnights with me: counting off the steps as we walked up them, playing games while she ate her dinner and while she took her bath. We had a plastic windup duck, and this toy would go into the bathtub of water. And then we would splash water, sing songs, and play until the antique clock next to her crib chimed 8:00 P.M. This hour was our sacred time: the eight chimes signaled that out play would be transported to Rachel's crib, where it would continue until she fell asleep. But that Saturday night our bath ritual was interrupted by a telephone call. When I answered a voice with great authority in it said, "Young man, I . . ." But I never allowed the voice to continue. I said, "Look, I'm giving my daughter a bath. Call me some other time." Then I hung up. After Rachel and I had finished *Goodnight Moon* and she had fallen asleep, I opened the Express Mail letter. It was from the

MacArthur Foundation in Chicago. It informed me that I had been awarded a five-year grant of $192,000. Later that evening the telephone rang again. It was Roderick MacArthur, who had been personally calling up the winners of that very first round of awards. I had hung up on him. I apologized profusely. Then I spoke with Gerald Freund, who was then the director of the Prize Fellows Program. I thanked him, but asked if public news about my selection could be avoided. I tried to explain to him the personal complexities of a situation that must have been a world away from his understanding; what to a white person would be an honor can also be, to a black person, the sense that one is being made a target in a society devoted to white supremacy. Gerald Freund just could not understand why I did not want the news about my recent good fortune to be made public. But I could remember, very well, just why I had avoided all publicity after, less than three years before, I had won a Pulitzer Prize for fiction. I could remember the contempt of a white colleague, who sneered intentionally in my presence, "Somebody around here is getting *too much* attention!" But Gerald Freund said that the news about the awards had already been sent out for publication on Monday morning. He said I should be proud, having been the first choice on the first list of MacArthur Fellows.

On Monday morning, I said to the caller from National Public Radio, "The gods are playful."

Later that week, I told a reporter for the *Washington Post*, who had come to Charlottesville to interview me, "I'm going to give some of the money to my church, I'm going to take Mrs. Julia Smith to visit her relatives more often, and I'm going to be the best father I can be to Rachel."

Mrs. Julia Smith, an elderly black woman whom I had met a little over one year before, had been, in those days, my constant companion. As a matter of fact, part of the interview had taken place at Mrs. Smith's home in Barboursville. Rachel was with me. I was holding Rachel while I talked with the reporter. The reporter later wrote that Mrs. Julia Smith kept saying "Moo" to Rachel. Rachel herself kept repeating "Candy."

Rachel was in my arms holding a lollipop when she said this.

Rachel remembers very little about those early years, but she does retain some emotional clues. She remembers the plastic duck, she remembers the antique clock, and she remembers the crib next to it. She also remembers Mrs. Julia Smith. Some years ago, I asked her who, of all our friends, were the best people. She replied, "Mrs. Julia Smith, Joellen MacDougall, Ellie Simmons, and the man at the Coralville Fruit Stand" (where we buy our Christmas tree each year). A year or so ago, Rachel, in high school, located through a library computer a copy of the old interview in the *Washington Post*. She sent me a decorated picture of a much younger version of myself holding her while she licked a lollipop. Through some miracle, Rachel seems to have escaped the extreme pain of that period.

But I did not.

I completed my last classes at Virginia, adjusting my schedule to meet the very powerful legal pressures placed on me. One of them was a list of written interrogatories, one hundred or more, and the very first inquiry was an accounting of all my books by authors, titles, dates purchased, places purchased, prices paid. I hired a student named Edward Jones to help me with the list. We spent almost one week listing close to two thousand books. But I taught well that last semester. The student evaluations, which were turned in to the people in the English Department office, were glowing. I know this because, for some reason, they were never filed with the proper university or state officials. Although they were turned over to the English office when my classes ended in May, in the late fall of that same year, when I had begun teaching again, this time in Iowa, some kindly soul placed them in my departmental mailbox and Edward Jones retrieved them for me. The students said, "Excellent." "He is the best teacher here." "He knows too much." My heart grew full when I read, almost six months later, these student evaluations from my last semester in Charlottesville. And I will thank, for the rest of my life, the person who made this kindly interference on my behalf. This angel must have been familiar with the destructive strategy then at work: hamstring the suspect, and then gossip abroad that he is crazy.

But before this strategy could work its will, I was in Iowa.

Before I left, even before the custody hearings, I took some things I had purchased for Rachel to her mother's house. Some of my former colleagues were there. One of them said, "*Who* do you think you are? You've *fired* the University of Virginia?" We were standing in the front yard. Rachel was shouting "Jim . . . Jim?" in imitation of my outraged former colleagues. I picked Rachel up and I kissed her. I told my daughter, "I will always come for you. I will always come for you."

Then I drove, nonstop, to St. Louis. I rested there. And then I drove the rest of the way to Iowa.

I flew back three times for the custody hearings during the summer of 1981, while I was teaching two courses at Iowa. Each time I was pressured to return to the marriage and to Charlottesville. I finally asked the judge to get the issue settled. But when his final decree arrived at my apartment in Iowa City, in late July, I decided to not open the envelope until after my summer school classes were over. The envelope lay on my desk for over three weeks. Finally, a friend from New Haven, Sherman Malone, came by bus through Iowa City on her way back from a camping trip with her family. We had lunch, and Sherman pleaded with me to open the envelope. She went home with me and watched as I read the judge's language: full custody to the mother, limited visitation rights, hefty alimony and child support, and lawyers' fees. In addition, in response to the largesse of the MacArthur Foundation, my apartment in Charlottesville, without any formal inspection, was decreed "inferior" to the home of the custodial parent.

Sherman Malone said that I got drunk and raged all night in my bed. She told me that she lay awake all night, in her sleeping bag in the living room, and listened to my ravings. Sherman told me, when I took her the next day to the bus depot, for her trip back to New Haven, that I never expressed any anger toward her. Then she left. In the evening of that same day, I went out to Lone Tree, Iowa, to keep a dinner appointment with Bob Shacochis and Catfish, Bob's companion. A number of young writers from my classes that summer were also at Bob's home in Lone Tree. But I did not feel teacherly that evening. Emotionally unequipped for small talk, I excused myself and went up to Bob and Catfish's bedroom and lay in their bed. Later, Bob came up and asked what was wrong. I disclosed a few facts to him. And it was then, during that bleak evening, that another instance of kindly intervention occurred. Bob Shacochis insisted that I go for a drive with him in his car. We drove slowly along the narrow, dirt roads of Lone Tree, up hillocks and down dales, through the dying summer light. Bob drove aimlessly past tall cornfields, past soybeans begging for harvest. We smelled farmlands and animal manure in the moist breezes of sunset. The heavy smells seemed to be insisting that one form of life was *intended* to sustain another form of life. The bursting crops said that this was Nature's Way, and that all of life was, finally, only an extension of this same blueprint in Nature's Plan. Kindly, cooking-loving Bob Shacochis drove me up and down those roads, desperate to find some way to help, until something renewing from Nature began flowing into me from those fields and I knew that I would not die. When we returned to Bob's house, well after dark, people wondered what had been wrong with me. Bob never said a word to anyone.

This was in mid-August of 1981, when I touched bottom and slowly began to rebuild.

I wrote to the judge, acknowledging his decree, and asked him, as chancellor, if the situation could still be moved toward arbitration instead of remaining in the legal system. He wrote back to me, saying that he was bound by law. He also suggested that I should return to Charlottesville, because the noncustodial parent and the child "tend to lose a great deal." I wrote back that I could not return. I also wrote my resignation from the University of Virginia on the back of the judge's decree. And it was here that my priorities came into clear focus, and it was here that I began to make some firm decisions.

I had about $3,000 each month coming in from the MacArthur Foundation, plus about $29,000 per year coming from the University of Iowa, plus another $6,000 for each summer that I taught summer school. In addition, the MacArthur Foundation awarded, in those days, an institutional grant of $15,000 for a period of five years to the institution with which I was connected. I had an apartment in Charlottesville, and another one in Iowa City, and friends in both places. Most important of all, I still had my imagination. I decided that I would not spend any of the MacArthur money on myself. The institutional grant, amounting to $75,000 over a period of five years, I gave to the University of Iowa Foundation for the support of young writers in the workshop. Jack Leggett and I agreed, over a handshake, that the money would be used to support any talented writer who, because of special circumstances, was not eligible for the usual areas of financial aid. I made a will, one leaving everything I owned to Rachel, and I named my older sister, Mary, Rachel's guardian, just in case something should happen to me. I tried as best I could to strip myself of everything that was a distraction to my focus. I began, then, in my *imagination*, to view the country as one big house. My bedroom was in Iowa City. Rachel's bedroom was in Charlottesville. Friends had guest rooms, for Rachel and for me, in Richmond, in Washington, D.C., in Stamford and in New Haven, in New York, in Boston, in Cambridge, in Chicago, in Oakland, and in Los Angeles. All Rachel and I had to do, with the MacArthur money, and with my own earnings after that largesse had run out, was to move from room to room in this huge house, bonding as we went with each other and with our friends.

It was then that I began to fly.

One weekend each month Rachel and I spent "quality time" together with Edward Jones, my former student, who lived in my old apartment on Little High Street in Charlottesville.

I hired a therapist in Charlottesville, one who expressed outrage over the terms of the judge's decree. He helped me negotiate more time with Rachel. He suggested that, since Rachel was older, she ought to be able to spend one weekend each month, and then one full week each month, with me in Iowa City.

Then Rachel and I began to fly.

The therapist suggested that, because Rachel was getting older, she should spend two weeks, then three weeks, then six weeks during the summers with me in Iowa City.

But, later, this same therapist declared that he could no longer do any more for me. He advised me to return to Charlottesville.

In 1986, after a court hearing, the legal system of Charlottesville conceded to me the full summer. I also "won"
spring breaks, including Easter, every other Christmas,
plus one weekend each month from after Rachel's school
on Friday afternoon until school time on Monday mornings. The lawyer who secured this "boon" for me noted,
with some theatrical relish, that the long weekend each
month made room for me to remain with my daughter
until time for her school on Monday morning. This, he
said, was the best possible reason for me to return to
Charlottesville for good. He told me, with some hint of
brotherly love, "Now, don't make yourself such a stranger
to Charlottesville."

I made myself a stranger.

Rachel and I met in Washington, D.C. We met in New
York. We met in Boston. The United Airlines people at
Dulles came to know Rachel through their escort service.
She told me they always said, when she was connecting
at Dulles for her flight into Chicago, "There goes Rachel
again." The ticket agents and security people at the Cedar
Rapids Airport also came to know me and our ritual. One
of the security guards, a woman, would always say when
she saw me, "There goes that father who loves his daughter." Rachel came to Cedar Rapids; I went to Dulles or
to National. When she was still too young to travel une-
scorted, I *imagined* a pathway for us. I hired Opie Porter,
Shirley Porter's son, to drive Rachel from Charlottesville
to Dulles or to National. My usual pathway was through
St. Louis. To reach St. Louis on the very first flight out
of Cedar Rapids, I had to get up early enough to drive

from Iowa City to the Cedar Rapids Airport to take the flight at 6:45 A.M. When I reached St. Louis, and was sure that I would be booked on the flight into National or Dulles, I would call up Opie Porter in Charlottesville and tell him to begin his drive. My own flight usually arrived at National at 11:30 A.M. The same flight back to St. Louis, and from there into Cedar Rapids, left National Airport at 12:30 P.M. During this hour, I would arrive at National, and Opie would arrive with Rachel in his car; she would be led to me, and then she and I would take the 12:30 P.M. flight back to St. Louis, then back to Cedar Rapids, arriving at 3:30 P.M. or so. Then we would drive in my car directly to my class at 4:30 P.M. Rachel would sit through the class with the grace of the innocent. And then, after class, we would go *home*.

Rachel passed through dangers. Once, during the Persian Gulf War, she told me by telephone that she could not fly anymore because Saddam Hussein had threatened to blow up the airplanes. She, like many other people, was very frightened of the Arabs. I asked her if she actually *knew* any Arabs. She said that she did not. I told her that I knew some Arabs, and that if she found the courage to fly from Charlottesville to Dulles, I would fly there to meet her. And then we would spend the weekend in Washington, D.C., and I would introduce her to an Arab. She consented. Then I called up Sam Hamod, an old friend, a Lebanese Arab with roots in Detroit, and asked if Rachel and I could meet him and Shirley, his girlfriend, in Washington. After Rachel and I arrived, and after Sam came to our hotel, I told Rachel, "This is Sam Hamod. He is a friend and an Arab." Rachel liked Sam because of his personality, but she especially liked Shirley. We spent a number of years, during many trips, exploring Washington with Sam and Shirley.

Just before Christmas, during a visitation period, Rachel called me from O'Hare Airport with quiet hysteria in her voice. A massive snow and ice storm had closed down the airport, and all flights in and out of O'Hare had been canceled. And since the cancellations had been due to the weather and not to any mechanical failures, United Airlines would not be responsible for meals and lodging for its stranded passengers. Rachel was then about ten years old. She had no money, and was being obliged to sleep in a chair or else on the floor of the airport with the other children of divorce, tagged like Christmas gifts, who were serving out their obligations to distant parents. I heard in my daughter's voice, that cold December evening, the quiet desperation of the many millions of young people who, through no fault of their own, had become casualties of two decades of gender warfare between selfish adults. In reality, the children had had to assume the responsibilities of adults, while the adults were content to dramatize their own fantasies. During that hard December night, I sat at my table and made telephone calls, like thousands of other anonymous parents, to every possible source of help. I called up Leon Forrest in Evanston. I called up Marshall and Irene Patner in Hyde Park. I called up a former student, Joe Hurka, who lived in a suburb closer to O'Hare than Evanston and Hyde Park. There is a kind of doom-filled desperation, if not hysteria, that comes when one realizes that almost every established structure of dependability—parenting, family, technology—can be rendered useless when the mysterious currents of life, or when the indifferences of Nature, decide to announce themselves. While the old structures still remain defined and intact and viable, the flow of life, which has moved beyond them, looks back at this impotency and laughs at the naivete of those who once placed all their faith in inventions of the human mind. I learned that night, or perhaps I only *relearned,* that all such dead ends are under the control of the gods of life, and that one must depend on *them* for magic, for instances of kindly intervention.

All of the friends I called offered to drive to O'Hare and rescue Rachel. But Joe Hurka's father had a tractioned car, and his suburb was closest to O'Hare. Joe Hurka and his father went to Rachel, while I waited by the telephone ready to comfort her if, by some miracle, she was able to get through the crowd of hysterical children and use the telephone again. Well after midnight, Joe Hurka called me from his home. They had arrived safely and Rachel was in bed. Joe advised me to also go to bed. He said that Rachel was fine, that she had viewed the experience as an adventure, and that I was much more upset than she was. He said that before she went to bed, Rachel had gone out to have a snowball fight with his mother, and that the entire family had been struck by her calm, politeness, and good manners. Joe promised that he and his father would drive Rachel back to O'Hare in the morning and put her on the first flight into Cedar Rapids. He advised me to go out to the airport as early as possible so that, when Rachel arrived, mine would be the first face she saw.

I did not go to bed that night. I waited until dawn, and after Joe Hurka called to say that they were leaving for O'Hare, I drove, ahead of the snowplows and the salt spreaders, to the Cedar Rapids Airport. When the flight from O'Hare arrived and when Rachel came down the jetway, I thought my heart would break.

Rachel knows very little about my side of the story.

A BELIEF IN the possibility of magic, or of acts of kindly intervention, has been one of the sources of our bond during all these years. I did not want my own pain, my own bitterness, to affect Rachel, so I intentionally grounded our bond in instances of spiritual nurture as a way of calling her attention to the possibility of magic in life, or perhaps I did this in order to heal myself. I just do not know. I know that, like many black males, I had never had a loving bond with a father. The void that this loss left in me was, when I consider it, a kind of opportunity. I was "free" to imagine the kind of father-child bond I would have liked for myself. I knew, from my own experiences as a child, *what I must not do*. But I did not know exactly *what I should do*. I was thus forced to improvise. During all these years, Rachel has nor wanted for anything of a material nature. I grew up in extreme poverty, and, as for all other children of poverty, the expatriation of this condition from the lives of our children is the first order of business, the first "Thou shalt not." But I wanted Rachel to exhaust her appetites for material comforts early on, and then I wanted her to look for something beyond the material world. I think I wanted, first of all, to open up a philosophical issue for her.

It is common knowledge that the human spirit has, for its illusion of stability, a sense of being totally encompassed, of being *held,* in a reality that has a structure of dependability. That is, all things *inside* the self and all things *outside* the self, ideally, must cohere, must seem to belong *together.* This is the gift of childhood, the gift of natural integrity that is basic to human equipment. I did not want Rachel to lose this gift, even as I flew with her over a corrupt and uncaring world. I wanted very badly to provide her with something she could hold on to, through childhood and adolescence, and as far into adulthood as she could carry the idea. Simply put, I wanted her to know that something *more* existed beyond the conventional structures of dependability. This thing had to do with, *has* to do with, the frightening vistas that come into focus when all things on which we once depended—family, status, settled orders—erode, and we are left to make a path for ourselves. During such times, when the gods of life seem to be laughing at our mind-based illusions, our only refuge must be in the realm of magic, or religion, or imagination, or in those instances of kindly interference that flow from the coveted goodness in the hearts of other people. This realm is beyond race, or class, or region, or all the other structures of social gradation. It ministers to life itself, to what is best in other people. I had come to learn this the hard way, and I wanted to pass it on, with my approval, to Rachel. *Something is always with us, in the darkness as well as in the light. And if this is true, then one must walk through the world, even in darkness, by the same light one saw when all was light.* Without really believing this, I tried my best to walk with Rachel through all the dark places as if I could guide us by my concentration on the light. This seems to me the footpath to the Great Road that would take my daughter toward some absolute meanings. As for myself, I could only approach that road by way of the footpath. Perhaps this was, finally, my destiny. But I wanted very badly for Rachel to leave the footpath I had trod for her and get on the Great Road that will lead, eventually, to transcendent meanings.

Perhaps, for this reason, we began at Disneyland.

The three great revolutions into which my daughter was born—the one called civil rights, the one called feminist, and the one called technological—had, as one of their consequences, eroded all accepted structures of dependability, structures which, in much of human history, had helped define what was meaningful in human life. A black person was *supposed* to be a servant, an inferior. A woman was *supposed* to be an appendage to a man. A technique was *supposed* to be something linked to ritual, and the ritual itself was *supposed* to be an affirmation of ancient, ancestral imperatives. Then, quite suddenly, all of this changed, and a new generation was left with the responsibility of walking its way through a broken world, one with no certainties and, much more crucial, one with no real purchase on the future. The fear and the anger and the defensivenesses that resulted from this massive break-

down has caused those who were supposed to be inno-
cents, those who were supposed to be the saving remnants,
the future generations, to retreat in fear from the world
that has been made for them. They seem to not want the
future, because they cannot yet see themselves at home in
it. Newspaper accounts, daily, provide stories about young
people in all regions and groups and classes acting out this
sense of spiritual impotence. Stories of killings in Iowa, in
New Jersey, in New York, in Mississippi. And closer to
home, my daughter recently told me that a young woman
she knew, named Elizabeth, had hanged herself. She was
a brilliant young woman, was about to graduate at the top
of her class, had everything going for her. And yet she
hanged herself, without telling any of her friends that she
was in extreme pain. And it is here that I want to believe
that some of what I have been trying to pass on to Rachel
may have been effective. Rachel tells me that, ever since
Elizabeth's suicide, she has taken it upon herself to write
letters to all her friends, letting them know that she will
be there for them if they are ever in that kind of deep
despair. Rachel, I want to believe, has learned about the
magic that derives from instances of kindly intervention.
She has learned this, I want to believe, from the sense of
magic that has been cultivated between the two of us, over
the past eighteen years. We have gone to Disneyland, a
place where the established order of dependability soars
up into fields of magic. Perhaps Rachel has seen, in that
Magic Kingdom, the places at which the rational world,
with all its assaults, and the irrational world, with all its
potency, meet and dance in some kind of benign compro-

mise about the hidden gods of life and their intentions. I
do not know. I do know that I have tried, despite my own
pain, to take my daughter along the footpath leading to
this Great Road.

We went to Disneyland many times and in many different ways.

We began with fireflies. We began with sitting on the
back steps, on the front steps, of our house in Iowa City,
always at dusk, and watching motes of light scramble and
blink in hurried conversation about their hidden secrets.
My girlfriend helped deepen this mood. Her name was
Vera. She was less than two feet tall, and she lived under
my dining room table. She only came out at night, and
even then she disclosed herself only to me. A magic tree
soon grew up just outside Rachel's bedroom window. It
was in secret communication with a magic rock we found
by sheer luck. If one wished sincerely enough for something, while holding the magic rock, that thing wished
for sometimes appeared, overnight, on the branches of or
under the magic tree. We attended church. Almost every
Christmas Eve, when Rachel was with me, Santa would
call from some point on his journey to speak with us and
to determine whether we were being good. We always
wrote letters to him and to Mrs. Claus, wishing them
well. Fresh food—carrots, eggnog, peanuts, candies—
were left on the windowsill just behind our Fraser fir, our
sweet-smelling Christmas tree. Santa and his crew always
had a feast. They always left us many great gifts. The only
time I was slighted was when I wrote my own letter to
Santa in the braggadocio of rap lyrics. I have never, ever

repeated this mistake. The Easter Bunny, too, came to our house each spring. He could be counted on to leave bounteous Easter baskets brimming with choice candies. The Iowa Tooth Fairy came, once in a while, usually disguised as a pig. When the accelerating technological revolution produced the VCR, we considered this artifact benign, but only if used for a good purpose. We secured tapes of Disney's *Dumbo, Bambi,* and *Jack and the Beanstalk.* We waited breathlessly for each new Disney release. Once, with this same streak of luck, we secured a copy of Disney's *Song of the South* in a London department store. In a mall in downtown Washington, D.C., we located a store dealing with items for magical acts. We always went there to study the demonstrations, and we secured a great many devices. We spent the winter months planning, by long-distance telephone, our plans for the summer and for vacation trips in late August. Our watch-word was, always, *"When the leaves come, we'll go to Iowa."* We flew, on magic carpets, to London, to Paris, to Madrid. We toured the Tower of London, walked the streets of Paris, took a train to the Disneyland in the suburbs of Paris. We took a bus tour from Madrid to Toledo.

But most of all, for at least six summers, we went to Disneyland. At first we went by train across the Rocky Mountains and the Cascades. We flew to Los Angeles from Seattle, and we drove a car from the city into Anaheim. We went to *Dis*-neyland, diz, diz, diz *Dis*-ney-land. Then we went by airplane directly into the John Wayne Airport. We took friends there with us. Sometimes we stayed for almost a full week. We took Jarilyn Woodard,

Yarri Lutz, from Iowa City to the freeways of Los Angeles leading to Anaheim. Driving, I would say to my female passengers, "Let's go, *men!*" And they would answer, *"We're not men!"* We went to *Dis*-ney-land, to diz, diz, diz *Dis*neyland. We met friends from Los Angeles there: Cynthia Kadohata, Jeannette Miyamoto, Adrienna Woodard, Brenda Chadwick. Jarilyn Woodard, Rachel's best friend, always went with us; and her sister, Adrienna, always met us there. Once we went there with the entire Woodard family, Jarilyn's mother, Barbara, included. While the young people explored, Barbara and I would sit and talk about adult things.

The best thing about Disneyland is that the real world is left at the door. Nothing unhappy gets into that place. It is a controlled environment, one strolled and controlled by infectious illusions. Mickey, Goofy, Minnie, and Company are always visible in the crowds to remind people of the possibility of magic. I have a picture of Rachel, when she was four or five years old, trying to pull Arthur's sword from its stone. I have pictures of her hugging Mickey, Goofy, Tinkerbell, Peter Pan, Wendy, Captain Hook. We always stayed late enough to watch the Electric Lights Parade, one in which the entire product of Walt Disney's imagination, waving from lighted floats, would parade through the entire length of Disneyland. Thousands of people stay until closing time just to see this act. The adults among them, from almost every nation in the world, seem, at that special time, to forget that they are adults and glow with the magic of children. In that place, both imaginations and spirits are renewed. It is a place chock-full of kindly interferences. I have heard it said that Walt Disney was inspired by God. I do not know this for a fact, but I do know that we went many times to *Disney*-land, to diz, diz, diz, diz *Dis*-neyland, always looking for something.

Rachel liked the Peter Pan ride and also the Pirates of the Caribbean. I was partial to the Small World tour. It was an old ride, in boats, one that displayed in each carefully crafted exhibit comic hints of a number of cultures. I always considered this Small World tour an optimistic assertion of untested assumptions. The beauty of the ride resided in its stubborn insistence on something—all those nations singing in one accord "It's a small world after all"—that was steadily being called into question by reality. But reality, as I have said, had been banned from the park. Both Rachel and I liked that. We liked to be renewed by the old insistences.

A time of reckoning came, however. When Rachel entered high school, realities began to crowd in. Her peers began to challenge the authenticity of Santa Claus, of her magic rock, of all the good things she kept associating with Iowa. She got into a fight with one critic and was suspended from school for a day. After this she grew depressed. After Christmas of that year she told me that she wanted to come to Iowa to live with me. A month or so later she tried to do harm to herself. I tried, at first, to negotiate a way for her to get out. This effort failed, and so I had to mount a legal fight. I lost this battle. Now both Rachel and I were disillusioned. I was prepared to throw in the towel, to give up on all the flights and on the constant wear on my health and on my resources. I was prepared to let Rachel go. But then, in another instance of kindly intervention, at another point at which an established structure has asserted the dominance of its reality, a wise friend advised me that the currents of life are not, finally, under the control of *any* structure of dependability. She counseled me, in response to my desire to give up the struggle, "I would suggest just the opposite." So the flying continued, through all of Rachel's high school years. And so did the reliance on fields of magic. If *something* magical sensed that Rachel was frightened of the growing expectations and demands of adulthood, as all teenagers are, some magic beads and crystals might just appear on her magic tree outside her bedroom window. This was sent by the gods of life for purposes of reassurance. And so, during those high school years, with the steady optimism of childhood behind us, Rachel and I kept going to *Dis*-neyland. We went to *diz* diz diz *Dis*-neyland.

I have no way of knowing, now, whether or not this cushion of unreality has helped or hurt my daughter. The world is an unrelenting enemy of all illusions. But, at the very same time, the world is always in great need of some guarantors of the future. It may well be that Elizabeth, the young woman who hanged herself, had no such guarantors. It may well be that Rachel did not harm *herself* because she, after being educated into the power of illusions, had something *more* to look forward to. I just do not know. But I do know that something was learned, by Rachel and by her best friend, Jarilyn Woodard, during all those excursions to see the Magic Kingdom.

It was Jarilyn Woodard who taught this thing to me.

We went, on our next-to-last trip to Disneyland, with Jarilyn Woodard and John, her brother, and with Barbara Woodard, their mother. Fred Woodard, Barbara's husband, did not go with us. But all of us had a wonderful time, as an extended family, during those five days. Rachel and Jarilyn had grown up together in Iowa City. Even when Jarilyn was two or three years old, Barbara would allow me to fly with her to O'Hare Airport to meet Rachel's plane coming in from Dulles. Jarilyn's heart would break each time Rachel left, and it pained me to have to inflict this loss on her so periodically. Both girls spent a great deal of time together in my house. We played "Big Bad Wolf" together; I cooked for them; I laughed when they imitated me at my table, mechanically turning pages in books, smoking cigarettes, and drinking beer. They used to write little tomes to me about the dangers of smoking ("STOP In The Name Of Health, Before You Kill Yourself!"), and many times I chased them down the block, in mock desperation, because they had taken my cigarettes. I loved Jarilyn Woodward as I loved my own daughter. Rachel and Jarilyn grew as close as sisters. They *were* sisters when we went to Disneyland during the 1980s. And they were still sisters when we went there with Barbara Woodard in August of 1988.

But four months later, on January 10, 1989, Barbara Woodard had a heart attack. Fred Woodard called me early that evening and said, "Would you come and get the children? I have to go to the hospital. I think that Barbara has just died." I drove out to their house and found Jarilyn in a state of shock. John was down in the basement, kicking at the wall. I took both children back to my house. I put John in a sofa bed. I put Jarilyn in Rachel's bed. Then I prayed with her until she fell asleep. I sat at my table then, and waited. Around 1:00 A.M., Fred came to the house from the hospital to say that Barbara was indeed dead. Then we sat until Barbara's family arrived from another town in Iowa. While we talked, Jarilyn woke up. She came out of Rachel's room and walked to her grandmother and sat on her lap. She never cried.

But for several years after that, whenever she spent time in our house, Jarilyn would, at the least expected time, burst into tears. This happened over and over. Then, one day, purely by accident, I discovered a roll of film that I had neglected to get developed. When the prints came back, I saw a collection of pictures that had been taken at Disneyland in August of 1988. There were many pictures of the children—Rachel and Jarilyn and John—and there was also one of Barbara Woodard, one taken at the Denver Airport just before we boarded our flight back to Cedar Rapids. Barbara looked tired, but she was smiling. Some weeks later, Jarilyn was in our home. I showed this picture to her. Jarilyn looked at her mother, and then she began to laugh. I want to believe that she laughed because, beneath the tragedy of her mother's death, lay an optimism still grounded in the happy time all of us had had the past summer at Disneyland. We went to *Dis*-neyland, to diz-diz-diz-diz-*Dis*-neyland.

Rachel will have to tell me, years from now, whether all the things I tried to do have made some difference in her life.

MY DAUGHTER GRADUATED, as I have said, on June 5 of 1997. I had vowed, years before, that I would not re-enter Charlottesville. But the high school graduation date, as it approached, became a kind of emotional clock tick-tocking inside my heart. It was the old problem, the old deeply *human* problem. It was a commitment to the purity of an abstract commitment that had come to ignore the reality out of which the commitment first grew. It was in essence an emotional structure of dependability that had grown into something just as adamant and just as unyielding as the structure of white supremacy that had first caused me to leave Charlottesville. And it was here that *I* learned something.

The real tragedy of the history of black Americans is that we are shaped in part by the structures that constantly abuse us. We study the sources of those structures, their mental habits, and we learn from them. It is a truism that the prisoner always knows more about the prison keeper than the prison keeper knows about *him*. But the deeper human tragedy is that the prisoner, who knows so much about the prison keeper, runs the risk of *becoming like him*. There may be a certain degree of "equality" in this appropriation, but it is always *self-destructive*. And, ultimately, it is the prison keeper who wins because his one-time charge now generalizes his old guard's habits of mind farther into the future than the *life* of his former guard. This freezes the flow of human emotions into habits of mind that have already proved to be destructive. The gods of life must expect something *more* from the prescient prisoner. Perhaps this thing is only a refusal to impose on the future the smallnesses of mind that have been imposed on the past and on the present.

Perhaps another way of making this abstraction concrete is to say that I will do for love what no power on earth could make me do if I *did not* love.

Early on the morning of June 5 I drove to Cedar Rapids Airport and took a flight into Richmond, Virginia. I rented a car in Richmond and drove the sixty or so miles into Charlottesville. I located the building where Rachel's graduation would take place, and then I went to a shopping mall. I found a florist shop and I purchased one rose. Then I went back to the auditorium and watched Rachel's graduation ceremony. This was the first time I had ever seen any aspect of her life in that place. When all the seniors had been awarded their degrees and were marching out of the auditorium, I stood up in the balcony and walked as far down the steps as the railing overlooking the main floor. When I saw my daughter marching in line and approaching a place almost underneath the railing, I shouted "Rachel! Rachel!" She looked up just as I was throwing the rose to her.

Then I walked out to my car and drove straight back to the Richmond Airport.

I took the next flight into Chicago, and from there I returned to Iowa.

Rachel came to Iowa City, two weeks later. She brought the wilted rose with her.

Now that Rachel is growing secure in college, I still want to take her again out to Disneyland. We'll go to *Dis*-neyland, diz-diz-diz-*Dis*-neyland, just for a reminder of something very precious.

Gravitas

Suddenly from behind us a dark old fellow wearing a black
Cordoba hat, a blue denim jacket and a scarf of fuchsia silk
wrapped around his throat moved stiffly past on a black
seven-gaited mare. Small and dry, he sat her with the styl-
ized and momentary dignity of an equestrian statue and in
the sun slant the street became quite dreamlike. His leath-
ery hands held the gathered reins upon the polished horn
of a gleaming cowboy saddle and his black, high-heeled
boots, topped by the neat, deep cuff of short tan cowboy
riding chaps, rested easy and spurless in the stirrups as
he moved slowly past as in meditation, his narrow eyes
bright glints in the shadow of his hard-brimmed hat. . . .
a little boy in blue overalls exploded from between two
small houses across the street and ran after the horseman,
propelled by an explosion of joy. *Hi, there, Mister Love,* he
yelled. *Make her dance, Mister Love. I'll sing the music. Will*

you, Mister Love? Won't you please, Mr. Love? Please, please,
Mister Love?

　　　　　—Juneteenth

WITH THE PUBLICATION in June of 1999 of *Juneteenth,* his
second novel, a kind of cottage industry has grown up
around Ralph Ellison's name. I can imagine Ralph's
ironic laughter at the mythic allusions that have been imposed on his forty or so years of wanderings in the desert of the American literary imagination. One motif is
what has been left to "that vanishing tribe, the American
Negro" during the forty years the leader spent gathering
his sacred text. Charles Johnson, in the *New York Times*
Magazine, lamented the lateness of the text's arrival. "He
was engaging in an examination of America and race that
would have been so valuable to have in the '60s and '70s
and '80s," Johnson said. "If we could have just had this
integrated into the discourse of race in America. But we
didn't see any of this until now." Another is the mysterious fire by night that destroyed Ralph's summer cottage
as well as a huge section of the original manuscript. Another motif, this one offered by the critic John Leonard
in *The Nation,* is Ellison's inability to spend less time con-
versing amidst the tempting ambience of New York's elite
Century Club. "In the early seventies," Leonard wrote, "I
was an appalled witness at a literary cocktail party when
Alfred Kazin told him he should spend less time at the
Century Club and more at the typewriter, followed by a
scuffle on the wet street, from which an equally appalled

cabbie roared away without a fare, like the locomotive of history." And another motif is Ralph's stubborn dedication to a radically new, perfected form of literary art. Wandering in the desert, fire by night, the fatted calf, absolute dedication to a perfect form of Jehovah. These allusions have attached themselves to Ralph as easily as they once attached themselves to Moses. Like the media-inspired marathon mourning of John F. Kennedy, Jr., these allusions speak not to either man, both of whom were flesh-and-blood human beings, but to our own deep hunger for community, for intellectual and spiritual leadership.

I recognize, now, that I have also contributed to this mythologizing of a human being. Several years ago, I participated in a tribute to Ralph sponsored by the 92nd Street Y in New York. John F. Callahan, Ellison's executor, had been urged by the staff of the 92nd Street Y to keep the comments by all the participants brief. When my turn to read came, I just could not resist my own impulse to mythologize. I read a passage from Suetonius's *The Twelve Ceasars,* a passage touching the life of Julius Caesar:

> He was fifty-five years old when he died, and his immediate deification, formally decreed, was more than an official decree since it reflected public conviction: if only because, on the first day of the Games given by his successor Augustus in honor of this apotheosis, a comet appeared about an hour before sunset and shone for seven days running. This was held to be the soul of Caesar, elevated to Heaven; hence the star, now placed above the forehead of his divine image.

Now, two years later, I recognize the human truth of the matter. Ralph Ellison was a human being, a brilliant and generous and deeply dedicated *human* human being. He was also my friend.

Since the publication of *Juneteenth*, I have read a wide range of reviews of Ralph's last novel, from Jonathan Yardley's disinclination to review it in the *Washington Post Book World*, to Gregory Feeley's very cautious appraisal in the *New York Times Magazine*. It struck me that almost all the East Coast reviews focused on the mythology of Ralph Ellison, while papers such as the *Washington Tinies*, the *Denver Rocky Mountain News*, the *Oregonian*, and the *Seattle Weekly* focused mostly, and very kindly, on the novel itself. It was interesting to note that the musical idiom of the novel was better appreciated by those reviewers who were able to disengage the content of the novel from the myth of Ralph Ellison. The most "knowing" cultivator of the myth, John Leonard in *The Nation*, lamented that he was once bothered that Ellison "so seldom reviewed and never encouraged any of the other black American writers of his time, which was a long one." Leonard went on to speculate that this father–son tension was almost fatal to the development of black American literature. "He seemed almost to have felt that encouraging the children who cherished his example and struggled with his shadow would cost him some body heat. So he hibernated for the long winter and sucked like Ahab the paws of his gloom."

After reading this review I imagined Ralph laughing. And then I could *remember* him laughing. This last laugh took place in early April of 1984, the last time I saw Ralph alive. We were seated around a luncheon table at City College, after a ceremonial honoring Ralph. Michael Harper had stood and had displayed a wrapped gift for Ralph. He said, as he proposed a toast, "Ralph, this is a gift from your sons!" Ralph had laughed, but then had said to Mike, "Then you'd better open it yourself, because it might explode!" Ralph knew very well the burden that Freud had placed on friendships between older men and the younger men they mentored. I believe that Ralph never wanted to have children, daughters or sons. But he was a genuine and good friend to those people he nurtured.

It was Aristotle who thought the most deeply about friendship as a moral virtue. He distinguished between friendships grounded in pleasure and utility, which friendships last as long as pleasure and usefulness last. These two grounds of friendship are common. For Aristotle, the best of all grounds for friendship was what he termed "perfected friendship." This degree of friendship obtains when one person wants for the other what is good for him simply because it is good for him. He believed that only people with comparable virtues could sustain this kind of friendship. Aristotle did not mean equality of virtue; he meant proportionate virtue. He meant that each is prepared to render to the other what the other deserved. Ellison himself explored this quality of friendship with Richard Wright, his early mentor. From reading through their exchange of letters during Wright's years of exile, I can see that it was Ralph who was the more gracious and giving of the two. Ralph had this same quality of friendship with Albert Murray, with R.B.W. Lewis, with Robert Penn Warren, with Richard Wilbur, and with William Styron. He also passed along this model of perfected friendship to another generation: John Callahan, Michael Harper, Stanley Crouch, Horace Porter, Charles Johnson, and to me. Simply put, Ralph was generous to a fault. I think now that John Callahan was expecting too much from people who were captivated by the myth of Ralph Ellison, people who failed to see that invisible qualities, quite beyond literary chitchat, can still exist as expressions of friendship.

This is awkward. You call me Ralph and I'll call you Jim. . . .

AFTER RALPH'S DEATH, in April of 1994, Stanley Crouch told me that he did not believe that Fanny would last through the winter. Six years later, John Callahan told me "those sonsofbitches who used to eat at Ralph's table won't even call up Fanny now, so I am glad now that I began then to do what I could for Fanny." I had already learned something about the sterile nature of literary friendships, so I began to do what I could for Fanny. John Callahan and I decided to get her a VCR, and then I began to send her videotapes, the kind of classics that Ralph loved, and batches of roses. I went from Iowa to New York to see about her, and once my daughter and I took her to the theater and then to dinner. Once I went to check on the VCR and took her to lunch at one of her favorite restaurants on St. Nicholas Avenue. Walking with her back to the apartment on Riverside Drive, I remembered walking with Ralph along those same streets in the late evenings, after our talks, when he took Tucka-Tarby, their dog, for his evening walk. Fanny seemed very frail and sad and I worried about her health. The apartment was cluttered with books and boxes of papers, but it still felt empty without Ralph's presence, his gentle voice, his ironic chuckle. Fanny was living from one day to the next within this emptiness, so I enlisted Mary, my sister, in a plan to help Fanny out of her grief and depression. Mary lives in Stamford, Connecticut, so it was easy for her to drive from her home to Fanny's apartment on Riverside Drive. Mary began taking food to Fanny, meals that she cooked in her home—a turkey dinner at Thanksgiving, special treats at Christmas. Mary would call each week to see if Fanny needed anything. Mary offered to take her to church, for a drive, anything that Fanny might want to do. Fanny accepted the food for a while, but said that she and Ralph had never attended church. Mary kept going to see her. During one visit, as she was leaving, Mary pointed to the great piles of scattered papers, books, and boxes and offered to help Fanny sort and store them and then clean the apartment. Fanny got mad, Mary told me, and shouted, "These are *Ralph's* things. I have to do it myself, *and I'm going to take my goddamn time!* Then Fanny began to cry. She hugged Mary while she cried. Mary could not see that Fanny was acting out of a perfected friendship with Ralph.

Even good king Ancus looked his last at the light and was a far, far better man than you, you scoundrel! And

many other kings and potentates have died . . . Scipio,
thunderbolt of war and terror of Carthage, gave his
bones to the earth the same as the meanest slave. Add to
these the discoverers of knowledge and beauty, add the
companions of the Muses, Homer among them, their
only king—yes, even he was laid to rest.

—Lucretius, *De Rerum Natura*

SEVERAL YEARS AGO, Avon Kirkland, a film producer in
Berke-ley, allowed me to view a hidden treasure. Through
some miracle, he had obtained a film of an interview with
Ralph, the last one ever made, by a producer who had
been making a biographical film about Richard Wright.
Avon had all the scenes with Ellison that had been edited
out of the finished production. I saw Ralph again, sitting
in his favorite armchair and at his desk. There were many
takes of him, some blocked momentarily by the director's
chart. Ralph seemed to be trying to come to life again, his
vitality breaking through all those many frames and poses.
I heard his Oklahoma drawl, his ironic humor, his absolute brilliance. He talked mostly about his experiences
with Wright, who became his mentor when he moved
from Tuskeegee to New York. The one word Ralph kept
repeating was "envy": how much Wright's fellow black
Communists envied Wright's talents and his intellectual
ambitions. Ralph always laughed after he had used his
word. It came to me, then, that Ralph was still confront-
ing, toward the end of his life, the same human problem
that Wright has confronted all his life. It made me very

sober, in a very frightening way, that black men who had joined the Communist Party, ostensibly to win "freedom" for their fellows, still remained so small-minded, at least toward Richard Wright, that a flea could very easily perch on the bridge of their noses and kick all their eyeballs out. Wright had been wounded by his own people the same way that Ellison had been wounded. I recalled, then, the famous episode at Grinnell College in 1967, as recounted by Willie Morris in his *new york days,* when Ellison cried on the shoulder of a student after having been denounced as an Uncle Tom by a motorcycle-riding black nationalist. "I'm not a Tom," Ellison kept insisting to the student, Henry Wingate. "I'm not a Tom!" Morris attributed this incident to the ideological battles of the 1960s. But now I think he might have missed something, something very important and helpful in understanding the anti-intellectualism of the group itself, especially as it affects those, like Wright and Ellison, who attempt to think beyond, and to go beyond, what has already been accepted as reality.

If one begins to think of white supremacy as a structure, instead of as simply bad manners, one might then begin to explore into just what a system, an organic system, does in order to perpetuate itself. Central to this structuring of institutionalized inequality is the cooperation of some segment of the marginalized population who act, almost unconsciously, as watchdogs over those others who challenge, in whatever way, the status quo. Such people do the dirty work of the system—to keep violators in their place, whether in school, in the workplace, or in public forums. In other words, what precedes Willie Morris's account of

the attack on Ellison is a narrative about how the motorcycle-riding nationalist from Chicago had first expressed
disdain toward other guests at the party: S. I. Hayakawa,
Fred Friendly, Marshall McLuhan, and Morris himself. The
party was full of intellectuals, Ellison the only black one. To
any envious or self-hating black person, whether nationalist or Communist, Ellison would be the safest target to
degrade. Envy can be creative in some of its aspects, as the
ancients taught. It is far more constructive for the envious
man to follow the example of the neighbor who prepares
his fields for future planting very early in the season, rather
than to not follow his example and then, in the spring, destroy what the neighbor's industry has brought into being.

Ellison talked about the Grinnell incident when I first
interviewed him in 1969. He said then, "Some of these
people can be as vicious as the Negro Communists were."
He had been deeply wounded. I remember from that
time telling a young black woman, at a party in Albany,
California, that I was writing an essay about Ellison. She
stiffened and then said, "I hate that man!" But later in
the evening she approached me and said with great sadness, "You know, I don't really know why I hate him."
Since that time, I have had occasion to wonder whether
open-admissions programs, black studies programs, and,
yes, affirmative-action programs have been manipulated
by Machiavellians to encourage an anti-intellectual "third
force" made up of envious, narrow, academic hustlers
whose only real job is to sabotage those intellectually ambitious black people who just might compete with whites
for the good things of the society.

I do know that their experiences with Communists, black and white, scarred both Wright and Ellison. In Wright's last speech, given a few days before he died, he spoke of meeting James Baldwin and a white American female at a sidewalk cafe in Paris. Baldwin said to Wright, "Dick, I'm going to destroy you!" And Wright answered, "Why, Jimmy?" Then the white female said, *"He's telling you for me!"* Wright's letters to Ellison are full of taunts directed at the Communists: "Won't the Reds howl then!" he wrote Ellison in 1945. In another letter he said, "We ought to be a kind of continuous conscience for the Negro people. They'll [Communists] hate us for it, but they hate us anyhow." I was recently shown a State Department document that strongly suggests that Wright, while he was in the Gold Coast in 1953, informed on Kwame Nkrumah and the Communists around him. If Richard Wright managed to locate an ideological jurisprudence in rabid anticommunism, Ellison seemed to have located his own sense of transcendence in the passionate embrace of two seemingly conflicting claims: Negro tradition and modernism as aesthetic resources for his art. His celebration of the Negro idiom so impressed me that, years ago, after I had written what I took to be a good letter, I began using the closing "Negroly." As for modernism, Ellison claimed as his mentors T. S. Eliot, James Joyce, William Faulkner. Richard Wilbur told Avon Kirkland in an interview,

> He wanted to be more than a race spokesman, I think. He was so deeply a spokesman for modern literature and art that sometimes he would have been talking for an

hour and he would suddenly rather unconsciously come up with such a phrase as "but to return to your first question." He did this very often, you know, and you'd have thought you were just sitting having a talk with Ralph but this revealed that, in some deep sense, even with his close friends, he was a modern writer being interviewed.

I have no clear definition of what modernism is, but I know it was created by outlanders from the settled literary traditions of Europe—James Joyce from Ireland, T. S. Eliot from the American Midwest, Ezra Pound also from the Midwest, D. H. Lawrence, Henry James, W. H. Auden from England and Greenwich Village—who came to believe that European culture had lost its vitality. These outlanders were shaped by landscapes in which myths were still being created out of rich oral traditions (the myth of the American West is mostly a product of the late nineteenth century as filtered through twentieth-century technology). They were also nurtured by the study of the classical traditions of Greece and Rome. Many were inspired by two nineteenth century intellectuals who wrote about a return to the aesthetic of the classical ages for the resources to reintegrate aesthetic disciplines: Jakob Burckhardt, in his *The Civilization of the Renaissance in Italy* (1860), and the various writings of Friedrich Nietzsche. The notion of rebirth *(nostoi* is the Greek word for "return")* was said by Burckhardt to have revitalized Italian society, and so the look back by Eliot, Joyce, Pound, and others was intended to revitalize the decaying minds of middle-class people in Europe and in America. In brief,

the movement was about relocating the myths and rituals that would inspire the fusion of opposing aesthetic
categories—realism, romanticism, symbolism—into a
new wholeness, something that, according to Nietzsche,
had been missing since Plato in his philosophical specu-
lations inspired such divisions. Friedrich Nietzsche, in the
nineteenth century, had predicted that the cycle of history
would eventually return (once again *nostoi)* the divided
narrative categories to a sense of wholeness.

According to Ellison's own account, his first encounter
with the modernist world took place within the segregated
world that Tuskeegee Institute was when Ellison was a student there. This initial encounter took place in the Tuskeegee Library, where Ellison read T. S. Eliot for the first time.
Albert Murray has told me that he first met Ralph in this
same library through his name on the cards of the many
books he had checked out. An avid reader himself, Al once
showed me a picture of himself and his very young daughter as they posed against a very tall bookcase packed with
books. But Ellison had an advantage not available to Albert
Murray. As he recalls in the essay "The Little Man at Che-
haw Station," as a music major he was able to work with
Hazel Harrison, a concert pianist. He tells us that Miss
Harrison had been one of Ferruccio Busoni's prize students
and had lived in his home in Berlin before the Nazis came
to power and she had to leave. She had met in Busoni's
home such accomplished composers as Egon Petri, Percy
Grainger, and Sergei Prokofiev. It was her encouragement
that led him deeper into music. It is interesting to note that
Prokofiev was a close friend of the Russian symbolist nov-

elist Andrei Bely, whose *Petersburg*, I want to suggest, may have had a lasting influence on Ralph. It is also of interest to note that Miss Harrison had in her office manuscripts of Prokofiev's compositions, which she often played for Ralph. As modernists, then, Ralph Ellison and Albert Murray had another advantage over their fellow writers with modernist sensibilities. They both were on deeply familiar terms with what they both called "the blues idiom." So far as I know, Ellison was the first to define the idiom as an art form. He did this in his own very generous way in his review of Richard Wright's *Black Boy:*

> The blues is an impulse to keep the painful details and episodes of a brutal experience alive in one's aching consciousness, to finger its jagged grain, and to transcend it, not by the consolation of philosophy but by the squeezing from it a near tragic-near comic lyricism. As a form, the blues is an autobiographical chronicle of personal catastrophe expressed lyrically.

It is interesting to note, by reading the exchange between Wright and Ellison after he published this review in the Summer 1945 *Antioch Review*, that Wright seemed to have no idea of what Ellison was talking about. "The *Antioch* came and I read the article," Wright wrote to Ellison. "I think I mentioned over the phone that I did not see the blues concept: I do see it, but only very slightly. And surely not enough to play such an important role as you assigned it. I'm not trying to carp over the fact that it was a Negro expression form. I simply do not see it."

But Ralph Ellison saw. He saw that the American vernacular tradition, mightily contributed to by the vitality and the resilience of "Negro Americans," had thrown up an art form that was comparable, in some ways, to what the Greek dramatists in fifth-century Athens had done. Strife, to them, *agon*—agonistic conflict and competition as the basic driving force in human life—in warfare and politics and drama, was a norm of daily existence. So were tragedy and comedy. The tragedies of Aeschylus, Sophocles, and Euripides depicted the essential tragic facts of human life—incest, patricide, state law conflicting with moral law. To the ancient Greeks, life was tragic, full of *agon*. But to them it was also comic. And the two dramatic categories were linked. Tragedies performed during the day, usually during a religious festival, were followed each night by comedies grounded in absurdities. The two together, working to achieve some kind of balance, some sense of earthy well-being, provided what Ralph has called "antagonist cooperation."

The exploration of the range of the blues idiom became a passion for Ralph. The uses of the idiom for literary purposes seemed to be his contribution to the modernist quest for reintegration of opposing opposites. He had already read the "high" modernists, those who have been called paleomodernists. His ambition seems to have been to add something that was uniquely his own to the aesthetic conversation. *Invisible Man* was his first attempt at this reintegration. But what is at the basis of *Juneteenth* is Ellison's dramatization of the jazz musician as hero. In this novel Alonzo Hickman practices a kind of improvisational heroism in his nurturing and mentoring of Bliss. More than this, the novel merges the idiom of the folk preacher with the style of a jazzman. Ellison had great reverence for the individualized styles of such men. His old friend Charlie Davison, owner of the Andover Shop in Cambridge, told me four years ago that he and Ralph used to attend the Jazz Festivals at Newport. Ellison always tried to get a motel or hotel room next to one of the featured players, so he could listen to them practice before they went onstage. Ralph was deeply skilled in keeping his eye "peeled." He wanted to learn if the sense of style displayed onstage, before an audience, partook of the style that could be overheard during rehearsal. Charlie Davison told me that Ralph once brought the blues "shouter" Jimmy Rushing into the Andover Shop so he could purchase a tie. Rushing, a burly man, chose the thickest tie. He put it around his neck and then rolled it up from the bottom and used a safety pin to secure it to his shirt. Charlie Davison had objected to this display of country manners within the exclusive Andover Shop, very close to the center of Harvard Square. But then Ralph told him, "Look. Jimmy is the leader of a territorial bank back in Oklahoma. The people out there expect him to create his *own* style." It was this same sense of the importance of style, I think, that led Ralph to make Alonzo Hickman, a former jazz musician and a minister, the hero of his novel. I think he wanted, like any good modernist, to fuse the two different styles.

I thought about Ralph this summer when I saw a widely syndicated picture of people running from the mass shooting in Buckhead, the Atlanta suburb. The original picture showed a white man in the lead and a black male and then a white female, all running from the gunfire. Earlier in the picture's circulation, all three runners were visible. But soon the white man was edited out of the frame, leaving the black man and the white female to run together. The picture was apparently intended to dramatize the impression of panic. The white female's dress is running up her leg, exposing her thighs. But the black man is running with his thumbs up. It is as if his dedication to style is greater than his panic at that moment. I know that Ralph would have loved this picture.

"Craft to me is an aspect of personal morality . . ."

LIKE HENRY JAMES, one of his modernist heroes, Ralph Ellison had a mind so fine that no ideology could violate it. The most radical stance he took, given his own racial background, was his refusal to view basic human experience exclusively through the narrow prism of race. This steadfast refusal was the source of many of his problems, and not with just those black people who viewed him as a "Tom." Even the most educated of whites could view him with suspicion. I once attended a seminar at Berkeley taught by Henry Nash Smith, the Mark Twain scholar. When one of the graduate students mentioned an insight she had gained from reading Ellison's work, Mr. Smith said, "Ah, Ellison, he thinks he's white!" Mr. Smith later apologized to me for this outburst. Of course Ralph knew

he was not white, but he remained steadfast in his refusal
to be limited in intellectual and human range because of
race. He saw himself as simply an American, a product
of the complex history of black Americans in this society.
He knew that race, and thus racism, was the great obstacle in the emotional and intellectual paths of all black
people, but he consistently refused to allow it to overcome
him. Both his life and his art were deeply grounded, of
necessity, in *agon*. Ralph Ellison was a blues hero.

The stands he took were principled ones. When I met
him, back during the late 1960s, when antiwar protest
was at its peak, his reputation had been damaged because of the rumor that he was *for* the war policies of
Lyndon Johnson. The reality, as I found out, was very
different. Johnson, as part of his Great Society ambition,
wanted to do something to help the arts. Ellison had
agreed to serve on a planning panel, along with Robert Lowell, Paul Engle, and other prominent artists, for
what later became the National Endowment for the Arts.
But soon the antiwar spirit of the times caused Lowell
and others to boycott the panel. Ellison and Engle, in
contrast, remained steadfast in their dedication to the
project. Ellison told me, years later, that ever since his
work with the New York Writers Project of the WPA,
back during the late 1930s, he had been interested in the
role that government could play in the cultivation of
the arts. While the New York Writers Project began as
an effort to provide employment for writers during the
Depression, Ellison believed that Lyndon Johnson's attempt to revive some aspect of the idea, during a time of

great prosperity, was a very valuable thing. Museums and symphony orchestras, he told me, had no trouble getting private funding, while writers had to struggle. To him the antiwar protest was one thing, while planning for the Endowment was another. Ellison chose to help lay the foundations for the Endowment while others protested. He told me, "My politics are my *own!*" He paid a great price for holding to this stance, but the war in Vietnam is history now, while the National Endowment is still here helping writers. Ellison's sense of *agon* was unlike that of Ezra Pound, who also believed that government had a role to play in the encouragement of the arts. But Pound took the radical step of joining the Fascists. He did it, he told Benito Mussolini, "for my poem."

The path that Ellison chose was grounded in something more than a selfish dedication to his own ambition. If one reads through the interviews he made during the years when he supported himself by working for the Federal Writers Program, one can see how deeply embedded these exchanges with black peasants, many of them recent migrants from the South, remained in Ellison's memories. One interview, with a man named Lloyd Green, contains some of the seeds of what would eventually become *Invisible Man*. Another interview, with a deeply religious man named Eli Luster, contains some preview of the sermonizing voice of Reverend Alonzo Hickman in *Juneteenth*.

During the great IQ debates of the early 1970s, Ellison's true, finely balanced temperament became visible to me again. Because of a deeply wounding experience with the initial wave of this racial backlash, I had grown somewhat cynical and wary. I became detached enough to see that a racial reaction was being organized, or orchestrated, from the highest levels of the society. I saw the mythologizing of race as linked to a ritual that I named "the Uncle Biff and the Aunt Bop." Stated simply, racially motivated academics, Uncle Biffs, advanced the argument that black Americans were, genetically, inferior to white Americans. And then the Aunt Bops, sentimental liberals, argued that black Americans were inferior because of our environment backgrounds. No matter what position was more prominent, the debate itself caused the deadly premise to be carried forward. The real question remained as to why this debate, which had the effect of reversing much of the progress that was being made, was taking place at all.

The fallout from this debate affected everyone, Ralph Ellison included. There was a great need, particularly at this time, for some clarity of thinking. Ellison and Albert Murray, his best friend and intellectual partner, were estranged at this time. But when some black Harvard students created the Alain Locke Symposium and invited both men to participate, the two old friends came together. They joined other black intellectuals—Harold Cruse, Nathan Huggins, Hollie West—in a wide-ranging discussion of the errors that had been made, politically as well as aesthetically, during the past decade. Ellison was especially eloquent on this occasion, speaking to students who, before, might have viewed him with suspicion. In a brilliant speech, he sketched for them the place of black Americans as co-creators of American culture from the very beginnings of the American experiment. He said:

And speaking of language, whenever anyone tells you you're outside the framework of American culture and when they deflect you into something called "black English," remember that the American version of the English language was born in rebellion against proper English usage, and that the music of the African voice and the imagery coming from the people who lived close to the soil under the condition of slavery added greatly to that language. And when you look for the spiritual context of that language you can be sure that some of the passion for the unfulfilled ideals of democracy comes from the voices of those black and unknown bards, as well as from my mama and papa and your mama and papa crying in church, protesting in pool halls, cussing in shine parlors, and celebrating Juneteenth (that's what we call emancipation). The language of the United States is part of black people's creation. . . . There is no imagery of the great nineteenth-century writers which ignores our existence as metaphor of the human condition. There is no specifically American vernacular and language which has not been touched by us and our style.

I saw Ralph at his apartment in New York shortly after he had attended the Alain Locke Symposium. He told me, in strict confidence, that Derek Bok, the president of Harvard, had been so deeply embarrassed that the great IQ debate had been aided by Harvard faculty members that he had flown from Boston to New York, had met Ralph for a meal, and had offered him a professorship at

Harvard. But Ralph was wary. He told me, "I don't want to get involved in any foolishness," and asked me to go to Cambridge and assess what was happening. I went to Cambridge and spoke with Walter Leonard, who was then Bok's vice president for affirmative action. Walter told me that he had done all he could do, that the Harvard faculty had become polarized, and that rather than stay on in a token job, he was about to resign. I conveyed this information to Ralph, and, perhaps for his own reasons, he never accepted the professorship. In later years, as identity politics began to be the new academic fashion, I found myself wondering what positive things Ralph might have contributed to the students, to *all* the students, if, during his final years he had taken that professorship at Harvard.

The last time I saw Ralph alive, as I have said, was at the Ninth Annual Langston Hughes Festival at City College in New York. It was a wonderful gathering of people and memory, one of the most beautiful and deeply personal gatherings I have ever attended. Of course Ralph and Fanny were there, and Mike Harper, and Robert Stepto, and Bernard Harlston, the president of City College, who gave a medal to Ralph and called him "teacher to us all." A group of students, named the Davis Carter Dancers, presented a dance based on five scenes in *Invisible Man*. Their jazz improvisations recalled the rhythm of words, the profound symbolism, that have gone into both *Invisible Man* and Bely's *Peterburg*. Ellison's mind was on *nostoi*, on return, I think now, because he recalled in his speech his loving and nurturing relationship with Langston Hughes. "I must confess," he told the audience, "I'm overwhelmed not only because I have been granted this honor but because the occasion imposes a certain amount of symmetry." He then recalled that Langston Hughes had lived only a few blocks away from the campus while Ralph himself, a young man struggling to become *something*, lived in poverty just across the street from the City College campus. In his speech he tried, once again, to lay out his sense of aesthetics to the students.

> In our part of society, which is not always available to the more highly structured levels of social hierarchy, we *have* to depend on personal contacts. These *must not* be destroyed because they are our lifeblood. We communicate through language, through gesture, through inflection, the timbre of laugh, the cast of the eye, and expression. This is, in many ways, the lifeblood of Afro-American experience. It has not been codified—I tend to say "thank God"—but it is our task to codify it. This defining of what it means to be an American who is also black, and part Indian, part white, or whatever. It is at the core of American experience. We are constantly attempting to define ourselves and then backing away from some conclusions. . . . Now is the time and the opportunity through which we can extend the consciousness of the entire American society. And in doing so we will accomplish something that has escaped us. That is, we will assist other groups in arriving at some sort of vital connections between our ideals and our actions. We will make the dream, the ideals of society, a living fact in the land. And then we can get on with what is important.

You're going to discover that race itself is of secondary importance. Ah, but *culture*—that is what is important.

I am very, very happy, now, that I was asked to give my own tribute to Ralph *before* he made this impromptu speech. Our two speeches, like the published interview we "made" together, in 1969 and 1970, are *linked,* one by copyright, the other by sentiment. Of Ralph I said that day, among many other things:

> Rome, in Julius Caesar's time, was content with the tradition of the city-state inherited from the Greeks. Rome was said to be "blind" to the future because it could not move forward without first looking back for precedent. Caesar's genius led him to *imagine* that by making the provinces equal with the city of Rome, authority would no longer have to flow outward from the city square. The concept of the nation-state appeared first in Caesar's imagination. The price he paid for this imaginative leap was assassination. It was left to Augustus to impose, consciously, the psychological habits that made ideas and institutions, and not blood, the basis for membership in a community. Perry Miller has remarked that only two nations in the history of the world—Rome under Augustus and America under Jefferson—came consciously into existence. He also noted that black Americans and Indians were the only wild cards in the ethnic equation. The cultural factors imposed by these two groups were the only elements that kept this country from becoming a mere extension of Europe. Of these two, black Americans made up the only group that

could not look back to a time before the very earliest colonial period, the only group on this continent which created itself, consciously, out of the raw materials indigenous to this country's basic tradition: European, African, and Indian. I admire Ralph Ellison because he had the courage, when it was not fashionable, to stick to his guns—to confirm the complexity of his ethnic and cultural background.

> *"Oh, yes, Yes, Yes. Yes. YESS,*
> *Do you Love. AH Do you Love?"*
> *'Dear Ralph',*

DURING ALL THE years since Ralph's death, I tried my best to remain loyal to Fanny and also to my best memories of him. I declined an invitation to speak at his funeral, but I did attend the ceremony for him at the American Academy in 1994. I sat in one of the back rows and videotaped the many tributes to him. In about 1997, I was asked by R.W.B. Lewis to participate in another tribute to him, this one at the Century Club in New York. Henry Louis Gates, a member of the club, had arranged the event to help raise money for a portrait of Ralph to be placed on the wall of the Century Club. I was very, very busy with my teaching, so I declined the invitation to appear. But I did send Skip Gates a copy of my tribute to Ralph, and Skip did read it at the assembly. Now, trying to think as Ralph did in the modernist vein, I think it may be useful to recall the words I used then in order to provide a backdrop for the words I am using now. I wrote:

Just about one week ago I was having a good, soul-renewing visit with Stanley Crouch in Iowa City, Iowa, where I live. Stanley spoke to my literature class last Wednesday evening about the place of improvisation in American tradition. He recalled that during the 1980s, Ralph Ellison had encouraged him to watch for the persistence of this tradition in, of all places, a television series named *The A Team*, starring a man named Mr. T. When Stanley dramatized the conversation between himself and Ralph, he imitated perfectly the understated eloquence of Ellison's voice. I sat with the students and listened to Stanley's re-articulation of Ellison's ideas, and I realized that I miss him, and still grieve for him, much more than I had cared to admit to myself. Ellison's voice had been an intellectual lifeline for me, as well as for a great number of people, during the Golden Age of this American century.

The hint from Stanley encouraged me to listen again to Ellison's voice. Ever since his death in April of 1994, I have been trying, and failing, to pull together my *thoughts and feelings* about this extraordinarily generous mentor and friend. By the time Stanley arrived in Iowa City, I had written more than two legal pads full of praises of Ellison's ideas. But all those pages were lifeless, I realized now, because until Stanley came, I had never dared to listen again to the tapes of Ellison's real voice, tapes I had collected in an interview with him in 1969 and 1970, and the tapes of a few of his lectures, which I had attended. Stanley helped me break this emotional impasse, and so last Wednesday night I went down to the basement and located those tapes and listened to them, and knew Ralph again as I had once known him: cautioning, suggesting, probing, ironic, laughing, humanly aware, unfailingly eloquent. I grew excited again, almost as excited as I had been when I first heard that voice in the summer of 1969. I copied for Stanley a tape of a speech by Ellison, at the University of Virginia, back in 1978. Then I copied a tape by Albert Murray speaking at Brown University during the early 1970s. I gave both tapes to Stanley, because these two men, their two mentoring voices, were, and still are, inseparable in my memories, as they probably are in Stanley's.

The essay that I am writing about Ralph Ellison I am calling "Gravitas." This word has been so bandied about in recent years by politicians and pundits that I was tempted, as an American Negro (in Ellison's phrase), to "steal" it and to make it my own in terms of meaning. I can imagine Ralph's ironic laughter when I use that old-fashioned description of black Americans. He knew the hidden joke. If, as he suggested, the American Negro was a new form of human expression created on this continent, he also knew Henry James's insistence that "form takes!" Secure in this ironic certainty, Ralph might even approve my efforts to link him to the ancient Latins, especially those of the *Res Publica Romana,* the Roman Thing.

Virgil, in his *Aeneid,* tells Augustus, and also tells us, that the Roman legacy is what Ralph Ellison once said was a hidden name and a complex fate. Both men spoke of the connection between history and destiny, of the relationship between past and future. If to Ellison the essential ritual gesture of American tradition was the signing of the Declaration of Independence and the drafting of the Constitution, to Virgil's Rome it was the circumstances surrounding the flight of Aeneas from burning Troy. Both writers, many centuries apart in time, counseled *piatas* as one cementing value in their societies. Aeneas leaves Troy bearing his father Anchises on his back (who in turn is bearing the Household Gods) and Aeneas is holding his son, Ascanius, by the hand and is leading a small community of people. This community of people will, centuries later, lay the foundation of the *communitas* named Rome. Virgil thus teaches Augustus that it is piety toward the ancestors, toward the gods, toward the family, and toward the community that has in the past, and will in the future, keep Rome vital. It is the self-negating of the individual will, Virgil taught, and the subscription to *religio,* to the binding forces, which result in *communitas,* that best describes *pias Aeneas.* When a man is in harmony with all these forces, he may have "weight," "consequence," that intrinsic quality named "gravitas."

During all of his writing life, Ralph Ellison insisted, sometimes to the extent of irritating some people, on the importance of *piatas* toward what the founding documents, and what the American *mos miorum* (the traditions of the greaters) pointed to as essential for the future. Ellison's insistence on this was almost religious in its intensity. I can still hear his voice saying, "Things were not *supposed* to be this way!" I had always been skeptical of his liberal use of the collective "we Americans" and "us" until I realized that this language always presupposed a community of people, whether or not they were conscious of it, relying in one way or another on the *mos miorum,* the traditions which grew out of the democratic principles and the aesthetics which Ellison so eloquently defined. I came to realize, slowly, that Ralph was speaking out of a sense of *religio,* one based on the promise of democracy, without which binding the entire American experiment would fail. The great irony is that he made these assertions as a black American, as a person in no way exempt from the slights and scars which derive from racism. He possessed the emotional strength to look beyond slights and rebuffs and attempt to envision an aesthetic approach to an evolving culture that would move us all beyond race as the beginning and end of all discussions. I have the highest possible admiration for him because he held to this high standard until the day he died. If Ralph Ellison did not possess what the Latins called *gravitas,* then the term has lost the content of its original meaning.

I have been told that the ritual occasion for this gathering of Ralph's friends is the unveiling of a portrait of him that will be hung in the halls of the Century Club. I have never been inside your club, but I can imagine Ralph being there, and I can also imagine the ambience he must have felt being an equal among his peers. I know that if Ralph were alive he would rise to this occasion with all of his eloquence. He liked ceremonies, and he was dogged in his pursuit of their ritual basis. I wonder what he would say now, looking at the unveiling of a likeness of himself. I think he would find some way to look back on the origins of the Century Club, to the *mos miorum* evolved by its past members, and he would not blush to say that, given the magic implicit in the movement of American democracy, it was only a matter of time before someone of his complexion and his background shared a place on the walls of the club, even as he had shared the ambience of the club during his lifetime. Ellison would see this ceremony within the context of something much larger than himself. I can see the self-deprecating modesty in his face, and I can hear him speaking about his own background in Oklahoma City, his riding freight trains to college at Tuskeegee, his various jobs, the things he learned in the most unexpected of places. No doubt he would flesh out his biography. But then he would add to it that he might never have become a novelist, or even have been invited to be a member of the Century Club, but for that one thing he loved, perhaps better than himself: the American experiment in democracy and the "rightness" of its proofs. Ralph would find some way to put that *Res Publica Americana*—the American Thing—at the basis of his own achievements and then far above them in importance. If this is not the *piatas* written about by Virgil, then the original meaning of that old Latin word has also been lost.

Even so, during his lifetime, Ralph Ellison personified this word, as well as many others. Among those others, perhaps it was *gravitas* that he personified with an illuminating persistence.

"Si monumentum requiris, circumspice."
"If you seek his monument, look around you."

Ukiyo

. . . How one positions oneself in the world will always reflect to some degree the seminal experiences and indoc-
trinations of class, race and gender, but may also . . . float
above them, wondrously unanchored in categorical imperatives, mysteriously untraceable in derivation.

—Martin Duberman on Paul Robeson, *The Nation*,
December 28, 1998

IN EARLY NOVEMBER of 1998, after sustaining a fever for
almost two weeks, I developed a case of viral meningitis.
This disease attacks the brain by way of the spine and can
be fatal, especially to memory. I have been told that Jim
Galvin, a friend and a colleague, was sent to my home
to see about me when I did not answer my telephone. I
am told that he found me unconscious, that he called my

physician, that an ambulance was summoned, and that I was taken to Mercy Hospital. There I went into a coma that lasted eleven days. The doctors at Mercy decided that I should be placed in intensive care.

Rachel, my daughter, told me that when Richard, my brother, arrived in my room, my eyes opened wide for the very first time

But a friend in Cambridge, Jim Freedman, a former president of the University of Iowa, made a number of long distance telephone calls and used his influence to have me transferred to the much better equipped intensive care unit at University Hospital. When the doctors there determined that I would probably not live, a number of friends called Rachel, at her dorm at Tufts University, and told her that she had better come. Jim Freedman called my sister, Mary, in Stamford, Connecticut, and advised her of my condition. Mary called my brother, Richard, in Atlanta, and advised him to come. Jorie Graham, Jim Galvin's wife, was then on a reading tour. She mentioned my condition to people during her reading at Ann Arbor, and one of them, a former student and friend named Eileen Pollack, quickly made plans to come. I am told that the students in the Writers' Workshop prayed for me. Connie Brothers, the administrative assistant in the Workshop, told me that so many calls came in, and so many students went to the hospital, that the staff imposed a quota. Only Rachel and Richard were allowed to spend any length of time in my room.

I do not remember any of it.

Howard, my neighbor across the street, gave Mary, my sister, a loaf of bread and a quart of fresh milk when she arrived at my home. Howard says he and Laurel, his wife, had watched me carry a suitcase and a video camera to the waiting ambulance.

When I did regain consciousness, for the very first time in my life I had to rely on *others* to disclose to me my own personal details for nearly two weeks. There was, in my hospital room, a packed suitcase and a video camera that I had borrowed from Rachel earlier in the fall. Jim Galvin told me that when he had found me in my home, I had refused to leave. Perhaps I was so deranged that I could only be convinced to leave if I fantasized that I was going, once again, to see Rachel. Another friend, Fred Woodard, told me that when he visited me in intensive care, I had pleaded with him to help me get out. I had apparently tried to leave so many times that my hands and feet were tied to the bed. Jim Galvin said that I told him, "If you were a true friend you would cut these straps!" Rachel said I called the nurses and doctors "fascist bastards" (a line I remember from Lenny Bruce's routine "White Collar Drunks") when they refused to let me go out for a smoke. Rachel said that I was unconscious most of the time, that I was literally covered with tubes and needles and lights. Rachel said my eyes were swollen and discolored, and that she recalls my opening them twice. Once was when she and Marian Clark, another friend, were standing outside my room looking at me through a plastic curtain. I opened both my eyes a little and waved both my hands as high as the straps would allow. Rachel said the lights, when I moved, made me look like a Christmas tree. She said I said, "You are so beautiful!" The second time was when Richard was there. Rachel said I opened my swollen eyes as widely as I ever had and stared at Richard. "I guess you opened them so wide because he was standing over you and he is so tall," Rachel told me.

Ted Wheeler, a track coach, cooked a meal and brought it to me for a special lunch
Dentia MacDonald, a former student, baked an apple pie for me and took it to the hospital just after I had checked out
Jeannette Miyamoto called me from California
Suketu Mehta called from India
Indera called from India

To this day, I have no clear memory of any of it.

FOR MOST OF December, while recovering, I sat in a rocking chair by my fireplace in the living room of my home, trying to pull together the details of those lost days. The record of the interior persistence of my life existed only in the memories of other people. Their recollections told me that my sense of humor had remained intact, as had my smoking habit, my sense of duty toward Rachel, and most especially my desire to be free. Moreover, I could still recognize and appreciate beauty, and remained capable of opening my eyes wide if the image coming into view was potent enough to touch me at the deepest level of consciousness. As for my *own* memories, I recall from this great encounter with the edge only a kind of metaphorical wandering, or flights of imagination, or of landings, from the open heavens to the shifting sandbeds of the sea. Perhaps it was Richard's image in the outside world floating above me, the shadowy world that the Japanese name *Ukiyo*, that led me to sitting with some of my father's relatives, females mostly, in a living room in a place I know was South Carolina. We were discussing some disputed facts about our family history. I had promised to make something right for them, something that was of great importance.

*One of the nurses, after an embarrassment, washed down
my body and then hugged me*

I believe now that the promise that I made to those women had to do with my relationship with Richard. Before my illness we had been estranged for many years. When he called me at my home after my release from University Hospital, he told me, "You have so many friends. I was amazed by all the friends you have out there. And I told Richard, "That's what Daddy always taught us."

I was referring to the way our father, James A. McPherson, Sr., had operated even within the tightly segregated world that Savannah, Georgia, was during the 1940s and 1950s, when we were growing up. Both Richard and I can remember his believing that the entire system of segrega-

tion was a joke. He maintained many heartfelt relationships across racial and class lines. He possessed a generous
heart, but liked to drink and gamble, and was always in
trouble with the law. I have two very painful memories
of emotional dislocations between Richard and me, after
our father's death in 1961. The first is from the time of the
funeral, a few days after our father died. I was seventeen,
Mary was eighteen, Richard was sixteen, and Josephine,
our youngest sister, was fourteen. We sat as a family with
our mother on a bench in the Sidney A. Jones Funeral
Parlor while a minister preached our father's funeral. I can
still feel the pain his words inflicted on all of us. He said,
"We all knew Mac, and we all know he's better off where
he is now." The fact that I walked out of the funeral must
have hurt my family, but especially Richard. The second
memory derives from a time twenty years later. I had been
in his home in Atlanta, and we had had an argument. He
had told me, "Remember when I visited you in Berkeley
in 1971 and you gave me a reading list? Well, you know
what I read? Airplane repair manuals!" And I told him,
"Richard, you are an ignorant man."

Richard had ordered me out of his home.

*The code sustaining the world that floats at the foundations
of the world is based on predatory violence and exquisitely
good manners*

THE EXTERIOR NEWS in December 1998, while I sat by my
fireplace and healed, was about the impeachment of Wil-

liam Jefferson Clinton. Slowly, there began to form in the various media a consensus that the animosity toward Clinton had grown out of the unfinished business of the 1960s. That is, his public persona remained imprisoned within the popular images that linger in consciousness from that period: draft resisting, flirtations with drugs, sexual adventuring. It seems that an entire generation, those born a few years after me, still remained in the public stocks of suspicion. Those who mistrusted them most were older people, but there were also those of that same generation who had followed orders, who had done their duties, and who had remained loyal to convention. They filtered through the media the voice of Shakespeare's Henry IV as he reprimanded Prince Hal for his youthful dalliances with Falstaff, Bardolph, Gadshill, Poins, Peto, and with Mistress Quickly.

My brother might have been of this group.

I have always maintained that there were two 1960s, one for black people and another for white people. Simply put, the black people were trying to achieve full citizenship, to get into the mainstream. The young white people, having already experienced the loneliness and the uncertainties of middle-class life, were trying to get out. The black people came from tightly structured communities in which interdependence was essentially a matter of life or death. The white people came out of communities in which the myth of individualism had imposed a norm of habitual suspicion. The white side of this divide was explained to me once, out in Santa Cruz, by a very gentle friend named Don Ferrari, who had been an early inhabitant of the Haight-Ashbury district of San Francisco, before it became a commercial legend. He talked about the spirit of generosity and interdependence that the early residents there tried to achieve. I have since read an old book, based on a series of articles published in the *Village Voice* during the early 1960s. The book, *Moving Through Here*, by Don McNeil, details the noble ambitions of this wave of pioneers against the mythical landscape of the West. The black side of this spiritual divide, set during this same period and against the very same landscape, was told to me by Anne Thurman, the daughter of Howard Thurman, who was one of Martin Luther King's mentors at Morehouse. Thurman had moved to San Francisco to start his own "universalist" church. His daughter, Anne, then a teenager, had found employment in a bank. She had been the only black employee in the bank, and she received what she perceived as brutal treatment. She complained to her father, and the very wise Howard Thurman focused on the inevitable paradox in the quest for greater civil rights. He told her, "Annie, what makes *you* think that they would treat *you* better than they treat *each other?*"

Howard Thurman wisely saw that noble rhetoric must lead to steadfast human *action.*

Konomi Ara sent a message and then a gift from Japan
Takeo Hamamoto called from Japan
Benjamin called from Los Angeles

My brother and I grew up together in a segregated Savannah, Georgia. We had enjoyed a thin cushion of middle-class stability early on, when our father worked as an electrical contractor, the only black master electrician, at that time, in the state of Georgia. But he lost his status, as well as control over his life, before Richard and I were adolescents, and the two of us had to go to work to help our mother take care of our two sisters. This training to be supportive of others, especially of needy women, I think now, shaped both our inner dramas. Both of us have what health professionals now call a neurotic need to rescue women. But back then we did not understand the nature of the path we were taking. Richard and I worked very, very hard to get our family off public welfare. In 1961, when I completed high school, I was lucky enough to get a National Defense Student Loan, which enabled me to attend Morris Brown College, a black Methodist college in Atlanta. In 1962, when he finished high school, Richard joined the air force, with ambitions to become a pilot. He visited me once at Morris Brown College before he left for Viet Nam. He had been diagnosed as color-blind, so he would not be trained as a pilot. But he later distinguished himself in Viet Nam, was promoted in rank, and was able to sit out the last years of the war at an air force installation in Athens, Greece.

Between 1961 and 1971, a mere ten years, I had experiences on every level of American society. While in Atlanta, I worked part-time as a waiter at the exclusive Dinkier Plaza Hotel, at the post office, and at the extremely exclusive Piedmount Driving Club (of Tom Wolfe fame) in Buckhead. During the summers I worked as a dining car waiter on the Great Northern Railroad and was able to explore

Chicago, St. Paul and Minneapolis, the Rocky Mountains, and Seattle. I remember watching King's March on Washington, in August of 1963, on a great wall of television sets in a department store in St. Paul. I spent my junior year in Baltimore, at Morgan State College, learning about history and politics and literature. After graduating from Morris Brown, I entered the Harvard Law School. I worked there as a janitor, as a community aide in an Irish-Italian Settlement House, and as a research assistant for a professor at the Harvard Business School. In the summers I took writing classes. In the fall of 1968, I moved to Iowa City, enrolled in the Writers' Workshop, and completed all my coursework in one year and a summer. In the fall of 1969, I took a teaching job at the University of California at Santa Cruz. I lived in Santa Cruz for nine months, and then I took an apartment in Berkeley, and then another apartment in Berkeley. I had begun to publish stories in the *Atlantic* in 1968, and I published a book of stories in 1969. While at Iowa, I had spent my weekends in Chicago researching a series of articles about a street gang named, then, the Blackstone Rangers. I had met and interviewed, in New York, Ralph Ellison, and had just completed an essay on him when my brother and his fiancée visited me, in the fall of 1971, in Berkeley. Both Richard and I had experienced very different decades. He had returned to Savannah from Athens. He had then found employment with Delta Airlines as a mechanic. He had moved from Savannah to Atlanta where he had met, ten years or so after graduation, a high school friend named Narvis Freeman, who was then working toward her master's degree. He and this hometown girl dated, recognized that they liked each other, and decided to get married.

But like my eleven days in a coma, neither of us knew the internal details of the other.

I know now that, to Richard, I must have seemed a product of the popular images of the 1960s. By this time I *had* inhaled marijuana, but I had not enjoyed it. This was because a gun had been at the back of my head while I inhaled. A Blackstone Ranger was holding the gun while we raced along Lake Shore Drive in Chicago. This had been a test. If I wanted to observe the gang and write about it, the gang had to have something incriminating on me in case I was a "snitch." The Rangers had their own code. I had also been a draft-dodger. My local board in Savannah had been trying to draft me since my third year in law school. It did not seem to matter to them that Richard was already in Viet Nam and that I was enrolled in school. What seemed, in my own mind, to matter to them was that my name had been listed on the welfare rolls of Chatham County, Georgia, and that I had gotten as far as the Harvard Law School. Given the norms of white supremacy, this must have been considered "wrong." Moreover, on a deeply emotional level, ever since I had walked out on my father's funeral I had kept my vow that no one would ever say over my body that my life had not been worth anything. I had also vowed that I would never allow *any* circumstance to force me into the hands of people who might do me harm, as my father had been done harm. So I remained in school, communicating with my local board from Cambridge, from Iowa City, and from Santa Cruz. Finally, my boss at Santa Cruz, a writer named James B. Hall, wrote a letter on my behalf to my local board. "You don't want this man," he wrote with his usual irony. "I happen to know that he's crazy." This was sometime in 1970, when the Santa Cruz campus, as well as the campuses of Berkeley, Harvard, Columbia, and Iowa, were exploding with antiwar protests.

Beginning in Cambridge, when I was twenty-two or twenty-three, I began to have a sex life. But I was never a fiend. The old pattern of being a caretaker to wounded females had persisted, and so I rejected one woman who wanted to give to me emotionally in order to bond with one who was needy. I repeated this pattern in Iowa City and again when I lived in Berkeley. It took a very bad marriage to help me break this pattern. This experience also helped me to better understand some of the emotional and psychological damage that the caretaker can inflict on the person who is "rescued." It freezes the helpless person at a permanent point of neediness, and it keeps that person confined in this role. Although the act of rescue may seem heroic at its outset, the interplay between one's own neurosis and the human need of the rescued person's desire to grow can become a battle, if not an endless war.

But when Richard and Narvis came to visit me in Berkeley in the fall of 1971, I was very much unconscious of my *self*.

Richard Feldman came by with his juicer and several packets of fresh carrots in his backpack and made a glass of carrot juice for me

Stephanie Griffin sent me a tin of homemade cookies from upstate New York

Ms. Miwa sent me a Japanese calendar from Oxford, Mississippi

I considered myself, at that point in my life, primarily a teacher. At Santa Cruz I taught writing and literature to mostly young white people from the upper middle class. I was living, then, in the basement apartment of a Japanese landlady, in Berkeley, and I had a Japanese girlfriend. When Richard and Narvis visited me in that apartment, I know now, the only experiences we had in common were our mutual memories of childhood and adolescence in Savannah. We could talk about family matters, about people from back home who were still close to us, but Richard's experience of Southeast Asia and of Athens, Greece, contained strands of memory so deeply private that they could only be shared, over a great number of years, inside a close relationship like a marriage. My own experiences were just as private. But, I still want to believe now, I tried to do the best I could to bridge this gap. I had invited Ishmael Reed to give a talk to my students at Santa Cruz. I invited Richard and Narvis to drive there with us. As I recall, we had a wonderful class. Ishmael was full of gruff humor and street smarts, and the students were receptive. When we returned to Berkeley in the evening, the four of us went to a bar and talked some more. Then I invited Richard and his fiancée back to my apartment.

Greg Downs sent me by mail a chocolate orange

Opal Moore called from Richmond

*Stuart Harris flew in from Richmond and brought a book
on Japanese aesthetics and some cookies baked by his fiancee.
Stuart hugged me*

*Mitzi Clawson sent a box containing dried beans and the
makings for fish stew*

*Craig Awmiller sent from Oregon several CDs and then, by
Air Express, some frozen fish cakes*

I have now in this house and in my office and in storage
close to five thousand books. I left home for college with a
single suitcase containing clothes and a National Defense
Student Loan. But my love for books had grown the more I
read and the more I traveled. When I lived in Cambridge I
used to joke that I was amazed to see so many people walking pridefully into bookstores or reading books openly in
cafes and restaurants. I noted that where I came from such
actions constituted an open invitation to be beaten up. As
a teacher, books, back then, became my life, an extension of
myself. They were a necessity for a very special reason. I had
been raised in almost complete segregation, had attended
a second- or third-rate college, and had been admitted to
the Harvard Law School where I had been exposed to the
legal and intellectual institutions that governed the country.

I had left the law school knowing only two levels of the society: the extreme bottom and, much more abstractly, the extreme top. This was still segregation of a kind. Only the experience of reading, I determined, could help me integrate the fuzzy middle areas so I could have a complete picture. Paul Freund, who taught me constitutional law at Harvard, used to say that his students knew all the answers without knowing any of the basic questions. I think now that I was trying to learn the basic questions through reading so that, when combined with my own experiences, I could develop a national mind—a sense of how the entire culture, regional, ethnic, class, institutional, functioned together, as a *whole.* At the basis of this idea, I concede now, were ideas I had absorbed from conversations with Ralph Ellison and Albert Murray. I know it was this very issue of identity that caused the black 1960s and the white 1960s to come together.

At a time when black nationalist rhetoric had become the new political fashion, I began consciously bonding across racial lines. I thought that the real end of the civil rights movement—beyond economic and political empowerment—needed, if it were to succeed, a moral component that transcended race. It was simply a matter of trying to follow the Golden Rule. This was the open but complex and untested area that lay beyond access to once-closed institutions. It was the human problem raised by Howard Thurman in his question to Annie, his daughter. The search for this moral feeling tone was what the white 1960s had been all about. It was what Martin King envisioned would happen, would *have* to happen, after the once-closed institutions became open and allowed free-and-easy access to what was unquestionably of transcendent *human* value. These were some of the intellectual abstractions through which I faced my brother in Berkeley that evening in 1971.

I gave him some of my precious books, as I had given books to students and friends for many years before that evening.

My next-door neighbors, two women, plowed my sidewalk and front steps during the terrible late-December snows and freeze

ALMOST TEN YEARS later, this time inside Richard's home in Atlanta, the long-delayed confrontation took place. I was then going through a crisis, and it seemed that every place I turned toward those people I had known the longest, there came the same refrain, *Remember that time?*, with some inconsequential slight or omission on my part attached to the sound of an old friendship breaking. I managed the crisis as best I could, finally deciding that the only way I could survive, as a whole human being, was to make a break with those people who bore such hidden grudges. This meant, in fact, that I had to make a clear break with an entire region of the country. It meant I had to turn my back on my entire family. I was willing to pay this price. So in 1981 I settled in Iowa City, made a new home for myself, and in 1989 I went to Japan for the first time. I made new friends there, friends who came often to this country to explore its culture. In about 1992, ten years after I had left the South, two of my Japanese friends were planning to visit Atlanta. I called up Richard, and I asked if he or Narvis, his wife, would greet my two Japanese friends when they arrived at Hartsfield Airport. But Richard told me, "No!" He added, "Remember that ten years ago you drew a line in the sand against the whole South? Well, now I'm drawing a line against *you!* Scratch my name, address, and telephone number out of your address book and never call here again!"

A white lawyer, an old classmate at law school, agreed to go to Hartsfield Airport and greet my two Japanese friends.

I KNOW NOW that Richard had, by this time, good reason for this total dismissal of me. It seems to me now that I had violated the ritual bond that we had shared since childhood. Our mother had been very ill during those ten years, and it had been Richard who had traveled to Savannah each weekend to see about her. It had been Richard who had brought her to Atlanta to see medical specialists. And when she was no longer able to live alone, it had been Richard who closed down her apartment in Savannah and had moved her into his own home in Atlanta. It was Richard who had cooked for her, had given her daily baths and shots of insulin for her diabetes. And it had been Richard, finally, who was by her bedside in the hospital when she died.

I recognize, now, that I had dishonored our mother for the sake of a lonely principle, and since those years I

have been struggling with what I thought had been vital
in that principle. To make this clear, to myself as well as to
Richard, and to earn the forgiveness of our mother, I have
had to imagine the shadowy dimensions of the William
Jefferson Clinton drama that is now occupying so much
of public discourse. At its basis, as I have said, is the lin-
gering animosity toward those who represented the counterculture of the 1960s. But there was, and is, something
much more subtle at work. The moral energy generated
by the civil rights movement benefited black people like
Richard and Narvis, his wife. Simply put, a black middle
class, with some economic stake in the system, was created.
The proper ritual stance, for all such beneficiaries, is gratitude and economic self-celebration. But before the largesse
flowed, there had been a much larger goal, one articulated
by King as the creation of a "beloved community," one that
intersected, at certain points, with the communal goals of
the white counterculture. Both movements, at their high
points, were beginning to formulate an answer to Howard
Thurman's question to Annie, his daughter: "What makes
you think that they would treat *you* better than they treat
each other?" Both King and Gandhi, his mentor, would have
answered, "Because they have been practicing *swaraj*—
self-rule. Because it is only through wishing for the best
for others that can one become and remain truly human."
Aristotle called this special kind of emotional relationship
"perfected friendship." The Japanese term relationships that
are grounded in such natural feelings *"shizen na kamoche."*
I believe, in justification of myself, and also of my father,
that it is only in locating these emotional resources inside

ourselves, as well as inside other people, that one can create meaningful communities, even across racial lines.

THE SOUTH, AS I had experienced it while growing up, and as I had reexperienced it in Charlottesville, Virginia, during the late 1970s and the early 1980s, just did not offer normative opportunities for this kind of human growth. For me, the goal had never been economic success. For me, it had *always* been a matter of personal growth within a communal context unstructured by race. It is a very hard fact of life that there exists no such community in any part of the country. But, at the same rime, it *does* exist in every part of the country, among selected individuals from every possible background. But this community is a floating world, a *ukiyo*, sustained, incrementally, by letters, telephone calls, faxes, e-mail, visits from time to time. It is not proximity that keeps it alive, but periodic expenditures of human energy and imagination and grace. This is what I have now, as a substitute for a hometown. I find it more than sufficient.

This is the thing I wanted very badly to explain to Richard, my brother, after I came out of my coma.

There is a very peaceful spirit contained in a fire that is kept alive day and night and day and night and day and night

After our mother's death, Mary, our older sister, began to grow closer to our father's family, the core of which still survives in a little community named Green Pond, South Carolina. Mary began attending reunions there. Then she became active in helping to organize the reunions. Rachel attended one such reunion in Atlanta in the early 1990s, and several years ago I attended another reunion in Detroit. It was a loving affair. Richard was there, and though we were wary of each other, we got along very well. Also attending was my father's half-brother, Thomas McPherson, and his wife, Vanzetta. She is a federal district court judge in Birmingham, Alabama. Thomas's sister, Eva Clayton, was also there. Eva represents a district of North Carolina in the U.S. Congress. There was no sense of rank or of status among us. We were simply family, simply community. When I began telling jokes, Eva told me that I should never call her up in Washington, as I habitually called up Mary in Stamford, to recite my latest one-liners. She said that they might, if overheard, land her in trouble.

WE TOOK A group trip deep into Windsor, Canada, across the river from Detroit, in order to visit a station on the old Underground Railroad. The tour guide detailed the complex history of this station, one grounded in a communal effort that had transcended race. He noted that a great number of wooden carts, piled high with manure used for fertilizer, would stop periodically at the station. And hidden in the false bottoms of those carts, beneath the great piles of manure, would be fugitive slaves. We were all in good spirits, so I decided to try a one-liner on Richard. I said, "Richard, those carts are the ritual basis of our old Negro expression, 'Nigger, you ain't shit!' Only we have forgotten the celebratory tone that used to go with it. Our fugitive slave ancestors really said when they opened those false bottoms, 'Nigger, you *ain't* shit. *You're a free man!*'"

Richard laughed then, and the years of ice began to melt.

LAST YEAR MARY attended another reunion, again with members of our father's family, in Patterson, New Jersey. She sent me a news article about one of the young men descended from this line who, Mary says, is our third cousin. His name is Leonard Brisbon. He is a major in the air force and is the co-pilot of Air Force One. He is an honors graduate of the Air Force Academy and has won many awards. In the article he talked lovingly about his parents and their values, and about his family roots in Green Pond, South Carolina. His lifelong ambition, he said, was to go to Mars. I plan to travel to the next reunion of this branch of my family, no matter where it takes place, in order to meet this cousin. I hope that Richard will also be there. I know he would be very proud of how high this cousin in our family has risen in the air force. In the meantime, I am practicing a new one-liner, one that I plan to try on Leonard Brisbon. I plan to say to him, "You crazy Negro. There ain't no collard greens on Mars!" I am hoping that Leonard Brisbon will laugh, along with Richard. I hope both of them will be able to see me as I *am*.

I also hope to have a much better funeral than my father had.

Perhaps this is what, in my coma, I promised those ladies who sat in a room in South Carolina

Reading

To Mrs. Gertrude Keith and the members of her reading group

I GREET YOU on the occasion of the 85th Birthday of your Reading Club. Fred Woodard has told me your group represents a long tradition of intellectual curiosity in the Kansas City area. Any group of people who have been reading for 85 years deserves to be congratulated. I congratulate you on your lifelong determination to keep reading.

I was born in the slums of Savannah, Georgia, during the time of complete racial segregation in the South. The structure of white supremacy had been so successful that even some of our parents and teachers had been "conscripted" into policing the natural curiosity of young people. We were actively discouraged from reading. We were encouraged to accept our lot. We were not told that books just might contain extremely important keys which would enable us to break out of the mental jails that have been constructed to contain us. This condition, however, was not absolute. As always, there were a few points of light. I remember one teacher, a woman named Mrs. Beasley Thomas, who used to invite some of her students—those with an interest in reading—to her home on Saturday mornings. During these sessions, she would serve us milk and cookies and talk with us about books. I used Mrs. Beasley Thomas as my model of a "good" teacher in a story called "Why I Like Country Music."

There were other points of light. I remember playing hookey from school and spending entire days in the Colored Branch of the Carnegie Public Library. I read at random everything that was available. In the Black public schools of Savannah, we would always get the books that had been discarded by the white schools. These used books were institutionalized as a way of ensuring that the black children would never catch up with the reading skills of their white contemporaries.

And while the books in the colored branch of the Carnegie Public Library were also ones discarded by the white public library, those of us who went there did find *something* to read. I also remember the "white" Salvation Army store. I used to wander through its section of used books at least once a week. I purchased there a used copy of the stories of my very first mentor—a French writer named Guy de Maupassant.

You are extremely lucky in Kansas City to have never experienced the brutality of the segregation I once knew. I remember that those of us in the South used to be amazed by stories we heard about the Black people who lived so much better lives in the North and in the cities toward the Western part of the country. But I remember my first real experience outside of the South. It was in St. Paul, Minnesota in the summer of 1961. I had gone there to take a summer job as a dining car waiter for the Great Northern Railroad. I lived in a "Northern" Black community for the first time in my life. I met people my own age who had attended schools with whites, who had read the same books, who took for granted the same public facilities from which I had been barred. But these young people, my contemporaries, seemed to be broken in both ambition and spirit. They seemed content to find a steady job, to attend parties, to get married, and to own a house. I used to go to the St. Paul Public Library every day I was not on the road. I never saw another Black person there. I believe now that, somehow, despite the fact of legal segregation, the system had succeeded in destroying the ambition and natural curiosity of young Black people in St. Paul, even while it provided the illusion of complete equality.

I think that our situation now as a people is analogous to the situation I observed in St. Paul, Minnesota in the summer of 1961. We have all the legal rights, but we seem to have lost our will to use them. Our children watch television instead. They know all the answers to game show questions, but none of the facts of their own history. Many have become dehumanized by one-dimensional images. Many have lost the capacity to imagine a life *better* than the extremely materialistic one presented to them by television. Perhaps we have forgotten just why slaveholders once passed laws against the literacy of Black people, and why it was that very careful steps were once taken in the South to restrict the access of Black children to meaningful books. They [white Southerners] knew, as we have apparently forgotten, that the human imagination, especially the active imagination, is extremely dangerous. It is capable of projecting an image of the possible far, far beyond the bleakness of the present moment, and the best books teach this lesson. Our slave ancestors knew this. Restricted as they were to one book, the Christian *Bible*, they were able to absorb that one book, image by image, and to find in it answers to their own hopeless-seeming situation. They were able to project their imaginations *beyond* their present circumstances. For example, to the anguished question of the Prophet Isaiah, "Is there no Balm in Gilead?" our slave ancestors were able to answer, Yes: "There *is* a Balm in Gilead." Using the resources of only *one* book, they were able to imagine solutions to a deeply desperate situation, as well as to their own. Imagine what these people might have done if they had had access to the millions of books we all have access to now?

I think something tragic has happened that has caused us to break our covenant with the imaginations of our slave ancestors. Not only do we not read; we have allowed other to imagine images for us. We live in terms of images that are reductive and negative. Perhaps this is the fault of our writers. Perhaps it is the writers who have stopped believing in the magical and transformative powers of the human imagination, and so those of us who rely on books as models of what is possible no longer find them there.

Perhaps the readers among us, and the writers, too, need to fall back on the "old" books.

Thinking about Mrs. Beasley Thomas, while writing this, I remember one item from all those worn and aged books that were available to the Black children in my segregated Georgia school. This item was a poem, and as I think back on it now I realize, given our bleak situation, just how subversive it was. I can recall only part of it:

With a book upon our knees
We may travel at our ease
Visit cold Siberia, hot Nigeria, Old Assyria see.
Even navigate Cape Horn
Any pleasant summer morn.
We may climb McKinley's top,
Into Etna's cradle drop.
Visit Pennsylvania, and Romania, Far Transylvania,
At Thanksgiving pick a rose,
Spend July in winter clothes. . . .

This poem illustrates the "freedom" of the human imagination. It also illustrates its power. Someone once said that on the seventh day, instead of resting, God looked over all he had created on the previous six days and found Himself dissatisfied. So He created Imagination and gave it dominion over everything else He had created. Those blessed with this gift are allowed to stand securely in their own contexts and make bold and audacious leaps to establish a sense of community within another person's spirit. They are allowed to see the world through another person's eyes, to relate to another person's needs from *inside* those needs.

The reading of good books might be called "training" for this kind of human sympathy. This is the "power" behind our slave ancestors to affirm for the Prophet Isaiah what he could not affirm for himself. "There *is* a Balm in Gilead" they insisted to him, even though they themselves were in much worse circumstances. And this was the "power" of Mrs. Beasley Thomas, my old teacher, who had the imagination to project from some of her students, from within a bleak and deeply oppressive situation, a much more hopeful beachhead in the future, one that she or us could see, but one that she knew she would never share with us.

Like the first generation of slaves, Mrs. Beasley Thomas was one of my saints.

I think it is important for Reading Clubs like your own to continue to keep alive this tradition of imagining. I think it is becoming essential again that the Mrs. Beasley Thomases within our communities begin to reach out to the less fortunate among us and reaffirm the sense of possibility contained in the poem I have quoted above. Simply put, I think that we have lost a fundamental belief in the power of our own human spirits and imaginations to project adequate images of what is possible for us. We have lost hope, and have therefore lost control over our own futures. Our slave ancestors never made this deadly mistake. We need to relearn the first fundamental lesson they learned.

On Becoming an
American Writer

IN 1974, DURING the last months of the Nixon administration, I lived in San Francisco, California. My public reason for leaving the East and going there was that
my wife had been admitted to the San Francisco Medical Center School of Nursing, but my private reason for
going was that San Francisco would be a very good place
for working and for walking. Actually, during that time
San Francisco was not that pleasant a place. We lived in a
section of the city called the Sunset District, but it rained
almost every day. During the late spring Patricia Hearst
helped to rob a bank a few blocks from our apartment, a
psychopath called "the Zebra Killer" was terrorizing the
city, and the mayor seemed about to declare martial law.
Periodically the FBI would come to my apartment with
pictures of the suspected bank robbers. Agents came several times, until it began to dawn on me that they had

become slightly interested in why, of all the people in a working-class neighborhood, I alone sat at home every day. They never asked any questions on this point, and I never volunteered that I was trying to keep my sanity by working very hard on a book dealing with the relationship between folklore and technology in nineteenth-century America.

In the late fall of the same year a friend came out from the East to give a talk in Sacramento. I drove there to take him back to San Francisco. This was an older black man, one whom I respect a great deal, but during our drive an argument developed between us. His major worry was the recession, but eventually his focus shifted to people in my age group and our failures. There were a great many of these, and he listed them point by point. He said, while we drove through a gloomy evening rain, "When the smoke clears and you start counting, I'll bet you won't find that many more black doctors, lawyers, accountants, engineers, dentists. . . ." The list went on. He remonstrated a bit more, and said, "White people are very generous. When they start a thing they usually finish it. But after all this chaos, imagine how mad and tired they must be. Back in the fifties, when this thing started, they must have known anything could happen. They must have said, 'Well, we'd better settle in and hold on tight. Here come the niggers.'" During the eighteen months I spent in San Francisco, this was the only personal encounter that really made me mad.

In recent years I have realized that my friend, whom I now respect even more, was speaking from the perspective of a tactician. He viewed the situation in strict bread-and-butter terms: a commitment had been made to redefine the meaning of democracy in this country, certain opportunities and the freedom they provided. From his point of view, it was simply a matter of fulfilling a contractual obligation: taking full advantage of the educational opportunities that had been offered to achieve middle-class status in one of the professions. But from my point of view, one that I never shared with him, it was not that simple. Perhaps it was because of the differences in our generations and experiences. Or perhaps it was because each new generation, of black people at least, has to redefine itself even while it attempts to grasp the new opportunities, explore the new freedom. I can speak for no one but myself, yet maybe in trying to preserve the uniqueness of my experience, as I tried to do in *Elbow Room*, I can begin to set the record straight for my friend, for myself, and for the sake of the record itself.

In 1954, when *Brown* v. *Board of Education* was decided, I was eleven years old. I lived in a lower-class black community in Savannah, Georgia, attended segregated public schools, and knew no white people socially. I can't remember thinking of this last fact as a disadvantage, but I do know that early on I was being conditioned to believe that I was not *supposed* to know any white people on social terms. In our town the children of the black middle class were expected to aspire to certain traditional occupations; the children of the poor were expected not to cause too much trouble.

There was in those days a very subtle, but real, social distinction based on gradations of color, and I can remember the additional strain under which darker-skinned poor people lived. But there was also a great deal of optimism, shared by all levels of the black community. Besides a certain reverence for the benign intentions of the federal government, there was a belief in the idea of progress, nourished, I think now, by the determination of older people not to pass on to the next generation too many stories about racial conflict, their own frustrations and failures. They censored a great deal. It was as if they had made basic and binding agreements with themselves, or with their ancestors, that for the consideration represented by their silence on certain points they expected to receive, from either Providence or a munificent federal government, some future service or remuneration, the form of which would be left to the beneficiaries of their silence. Lawyers would call this a contract with a condition precedent. And maybe because they did tell us less than they knew, many of us were less informed than we might have been. On the other hand, because of this same silence many of us remained free enough of the influence of negative stories to take chances, be ridiculous, perhaps even try to form our own positive stories out of whatever our own experiences provided. Though ours was a limited world, it was one rich in possibilities for the future.

If I had to account for my life from segregated Savannah to this place and point in time, I would probably have to say that the contract would be no bad metaphor. I am reminded of Sir Henry Maine's observation that the progress of society is from status to contract. Although he was writing about the development of English common law, the reverse of his generalization is most applicable to my situation: I am the beneficiary of a number of contracts, most of them between the federal government and the institutions of society, intended to provide people like me with a certain status.

I recall that in 1960, for example, something called the National Defense Student Loan Program went into effect, and I found out that by my agreeing to repay a loan plus some little interest, the federal government would back my enrollment in a small Negro college in Georgia. When I was a freshman at that college, disagreement over a seniority clause between the Hotel & Restaurant Employees and Bartenders Union and the Great Northern Railway Company, in St. Paul, Minnesota, caused management to begin recruiting temporary summer help. Before I was nineteen I was encouraged to move from a segregated Negro college in the South and through that very beautiful part of the country that lies between Chicago and the Pacific Northwest. That year—1962—the World's Fair was in Seattle, and it was a magnificently diverse panorama for a young man to see. Almost every nation on earth was represented in some way, and at the center of the fair was the Space Needle. The theme of the U.S. exhibit, as I recall, was drawn from Whitman's *Leaves of Grass:* "Conquering, holding, daring, venturing as we go the unknown ways."

When I returned to the South, in the midst of all the civil rights activity, I saw a poster advertising a creative-writing contest sponsored by *Reader's Digest* and the United Negro College Fund. To enter the contest I had to learn to write and type. The first story I wrote was lost (and very badly typed); but the second, written in 1965, although also badly typed, was awarded first prize by Edward Weeks and his staff at the *Atlantic Monthly.* That same year I was offered the opportunity to enter Harvard Law School. During my second year at law school, a third-year man named Dave Marston (who was in a contest with Attorney General Griffin Bell earlier that year) offered me, through a very conservative white fellow student from Texas, the opportunity to take over his old job as a janitor in one of the apartment buildings in Cambridge. There I had the solitude, and the encouragement, to begin writing seriously. Offering my services in that building was probably the best contract I ever made.

I have not recalled all the above to sing my own praises or to evoke the black American version of the Horatio Alger myth. I have recited these facts as a way of indicating the haphazard nature of events during that ten-year period. I am the product of a contractual process. To put it simply, the 1960s were a crazy time. Opportunities seemed to materialize out of thin air; and if you were lucky, if you were in the right place at the right time, certain contractual benefits just naturally accrued. You were assured of a certain status; you could become a doctor, a lawyer, a dentist, an accountant, an engineer. Achieving these things was easy, if you applied yourself.

But a very hard price was extracted. It seems to me now, from the perspective provided by age and distance, that certain institutional forces, acting impersonally, threw together black peasants and white aristocrats, people who operated on the plane of the intellect and people who valued the perspective of the folk. There were people who were frightened, threatened, and felt inferior; there were light-skinned people who called themselves "black," and there were dark-skinned people who could remember when this term had been used negatively; there were idealists and opportunists, people who seemed to want to be exploited and people who delighted in exploiting them. Old identities were thrown off, of necessity, but there were not many new ones of a positive nature to be assumed. People from backgrounds like my own, those from the South, while content with the new opportunities, found themselves trying to make sense of the growing diversity of friendships, of their increasing familiarity with the various political areas of the country, of the obvious differences between their values and those of their parents. We *were* becoming doctors, lawyers, dentists, engineers; but at the same time our experiences forced us to begin thinking of ourselves in new and different ways. We never wanted to be "white," but we never wanted to be "black" either. And back during that period there was the feeling that we could be whatever we wanted. But, we discovered, unless we joined a group, subscribed to some ideology, accepted some provisional identity, there was no contractual process for defining and stabilizing what it was we wanted to be. We also found that this was an individual problem, and in order to confront it one had to go inside one's self.

NOW I WANT to return to my personal experience, to one of the contracts that took me from segregated Savannah to the Seattle World's Fair. There were many things about my earliest experiences that I liked and wanted to preserve, despite the fact that these things took place in a context of segregation; and there were a great many things I liked about the vision of all those nations interacting at the World's Fair. But the two seemed to belong to separate realities, to represent two different worldviews. Similarly, there were some things I liked about many of the dining-car waiters with whom I worked, and some things I liked about people like Dave Marston whom I met in law school. Some of these people and their values were called "black" and some were called "white," and I learned very quickly that all of us tend to wall ourselves off from experiences different from our own by assigning to these terms greater significance than they should have. Moreover, I found that trying to maintain friendships with, say, a politically conservative white Texan, a liberal-to-radical classmate of Scottish-Italian background, my oldest black friends, and even members of my own family induced psychological contradictions that became tense and painful as the political climate shifted. There were no contracts covering such friendships and such feelings, and in order to keep the friends and maintain the feelings I had to force myself to find a basis other than race on which contradictory urgings could be synthesized. I discovered that I had to find, first of all, an identity as a writer, and then I had to express what I knew or felt in such a way that I could make something whole out of a necessarily fragmented experience.

While in San Francisco, I saw in the image of the nineteenth-century American locomotive a possible cultural symbol that could represent my folk origins and their values, as well as the values of all the people I had seen at the World's Fair. During that same time, unconsciously, I was also beginning to see that the American language, in its flexibility and variety of idioms, could at least approximate some of the contradictory feelings that had resulted from my experience. Once again, I could not find any contractual guarantee that this would be the most appropriate and rewarding way to hold myself, and my experience, together. I think now there are no such contracts.

I quoted earlier a generalization by Sir Henry Maine to the effect that human society is a matter of movement from status to contract. Actually, I have never read Sir Henry Maine.

I lifted his statement from a book by a man named Henry Allen Moe—a great book called *The Power of Freedom*. In that book, in an essay entitled "The Future of Liberal Arts Education," Moe goes on to say that a next step, one that goes beyond contract, is now necessary, but that no one seems to know what that next step should be. Certain trends suggest that it may well be a reversion to status. But if this happens it will be a tragedy of major proportions, because most of the people in the world are waiting for some nation, some people, to provide the model for the next step. And somehow I felt, while writing the last stories in *Elbow Room,* that what the old folks in my hometown wanted in exchange for their censoring was not just status of a conventional kind. I want to think that after having waited so long, after having seen so much, they must have at least expected some new stories that would no longer have to be censored to come out of our experience. I felt that if anything, the long experience of segregation could be looked on as a period of preparation for a next step. Those of us who are black and who have had to defend our humanity should be obliged to continue defending it, on higher and higher levels—not of power, which is a kind of tragic trap, but on higher levels of consciousness.

All of this is being said in retrospect, and I am quite aware that I am rationalizing many complex and contradictory feelings. Nevertheless, I do know that early on, during my second year of law school, I became conscious of a model of identity that might help me transcend, at least in my thinking, a provisional or racial identity. In a class in American constitutional law taught by Paul Freund, I began to play with the idea that the Fourteenth Amendment was not just a legislative instrument devised to give former slaves legal equality with other Americans. Looking at the slow but steady way in which the basic guarantees of the Bill of Rights had, through judicial interpretation, been incorporated into the clauses of that amendment, I began to see the outlines of a new identity.

You will recall that the first line of Section 1 of the Fourteenth Amendment makes an all-inclusive definition of citizenship: "All persons born or naturalized in the United States, and subject to the jurisdiction thereof, are citizens of the United States. . . ." The rights guaranteed to such a citizen had themselves traveled from the provinces to the World's Fair: from the trial and error of early Anglo-Saxon folk rituals to the rights of freemen established by the Magna Carta, to their slow incorporation into early American colonial charters, and from these charters (especially Virginia's Bill of Rights, written by George Mason) into the U.S. Constitution as its first ten amendments. Indeed, these same rights had served as the basis for the Charter of the United Nations. I saw that through the protean uses made of the Fourteenth Amendment, in the gradual elaboration of basic rights to be protected by federal authority, an outline of something much more complex than "black" and "white" had been begun.

It was many years before I was to go to the Library of Congress and read the brief of the lawyer-novelist Albion W. Tourgee in the famous case *Plessy* v. *Ferguson*. Argued in 1896 before the United States Supreme Court, Tourgee's brief was the first meaningful attempt to breathe life into the amendment. I will quote here part of his brief, which is a very beautiful piece of literature:

> This provision of Section I of the Fourteenth Amendment *creates* a new citizenship of the United States embracing *new* rights, privileges and immunities, derivable in a *new* manner, controlled by *new* authority, having a *new* scope and extent, depending on national authority

for its existence and looking to national power for its preservation.

Although Tourgee lost the argument before the Supreme Court, his model of citizenship—and it is not a racial one—is still the most radical idea to come out of American constitutional law. He provided the outline, the clothing, if you will, for a new level of status. What he was proposing in 1896, I think, was that each United States citizen would attempt to approximate the ideals of the nation, be on at least conversant terms with all its diversity, carry the mainstream of the culture inside himself. As an American, by trying to wear these clothes he would be a synthesis of high and low, black and white, city and country, provincial and universal. If he could live with these contradictions, he would be simply a representative American.

This was the model I was aiming for in my book of stories. It can be achieved with or without intermarriage, but it will cost a great many mistakes and a lot of pain. It is, finally, a product of culture and not of race. And achieving it will require that one be conscious of America's culture and the complexity of all its people. As I tried to point out, such a perspective would provide a minefield of delicious ironies. Why, for example, should black Americans raised in southern culture *not* find that some of their responses are geared to country music? How else, except in terms of cultural diversity, am I to account for the white friend in Boston who taught me much of what I know about black American music? Or the white friend in Virginia who, besides developing a homegrown aesthetic he calls "crackertude," knows more about black American folklore than most black people? Or the possibility that many black people in Los Angeles have been just as much influenced by Hollywood's "star system" of the forties and fifties as they have been by society's response to the color of their skins? I wrote about people like these in *Elbow Room* because they interested me, and because they help support my belief that most of us are products of much more complex cultural influences than we suppose.

WHAT I HAVE said above will make little sense until certain contradictions in the nation's background are faced up to, until personal identities are allowed to partake of the complexity of the country's history as well as of its culture. Some years ago, a very imaginative black comedian named Richard Pryor appeared briefly on national television in his own show. He offended a great many people, and his show was canceled after only a few weeks. But I remember one episode that may emphasize my own group's confusion about its historical experience. This was a satiric takeoff on the popular television movie *Roots,* and Pryor played an African tribal historian who was selling trinkets and impromptu history to black American tourists. One tourist, a middle-class man, approached the tribal historian and said, "I want you to tell me who my great-great-granddaddy was." The African handed him a picture. The black American looked at it and said, "But that's a *white* man!" The tribal historian said, "That's right." Then the tourist said, "Well, I want you to tell me where I'm from." The historian looked hard at him and said, "You're from Cleveland, nigger." I think I was trying very hard in my book to say the same thing, but not just to black people.

Today I am not the lawyer my friend in San Francisco thought I should be, but this is the record I wanted to present to him that rainy evening back in 1974. It may illustrate why the terms of my acceptance of society's offer had to be modified. I am now a writer, a person who has to learn to live with contradictions, frustrations, and doubts. Still, I have another quote that sustains me, this one from a book called *The Tragic Sense of Life,* by the Spanish philosopher Miguel de Unamuno. In a chapter called "Don Quixote Today" Unamuno asks, "How is it that among the words the English have borrowed from our language there is to be this word *desperado?*" And he answers himself: "It is despair, and despair alone, that begets heroic hope, absurd hope, mad hope."

I believe that the United States is complex enough to induce that sort of despair that begets heroic hope. I believe that if one can experience its diversity, touch a variety of its people, laugh at its craziness, distill wisdom from its tragedies, attempt to synthesize all this inside oneself without going crazy, one will have earned twountant. If nothing else, one will have learned a few new stories and, most important, one will have begun on that necessary movement from contract to the next step, from province to the World's Fair, from a hopeless person to a desperado.

I wrote about my first uncertain steps in this direction in *Elbow Room* because I have benefited from all the contracts, I have exhausted all the contracts, and at present it is the only new direction I know.

ACKNOWLEDGMENTS

Thank you to Jan Weissmiller at Prairie Lights Books and Lan Samantha Chang at the Iowa Writers' Workshop for advice along the way. To Allen Gee for his continued dedication to my dad, his friend and mentor. To Joshua Bodwell for his patience and thoughtfulness. And all my gratitude to Anthony Walton, whose vision and insight shepherded this project into being, and whose rich understanding of my dad will help others appreciate his work more deeply. —R.M.

Thank you to Rachel McPherson, Allen Gee, Heather Treseler, and Dewitt Henry for trust, support, and belief in this project. —A.W.

The publisher wishes to express their deepest gratitude to Rachel McPherson, without whom this book would not exist.

"Ivy Day in the Empty Room" first appeared in *The Iowa Review*, Vol. 23, Issue 3, 1993.
"To Blacks and Jews: Hab Rachmones" first appeared in *Tikkun*, Vol. 4, No. 5, 1989.
"The New Comic Style of Richard Pryor" first appeared in *The New York Times* on April 27, 1975.
"Crabcakes" first appeared in *DoubleTake*, Issue 1, 1995, and was later collected in *The Best American Essays* in 1996.
"Disneyland" first appeared in *Fathering Daughters: Reflections by Men* (Beacon Press, 1998), co-edited by McPherson and Dewitt Henry; it was later collected in McPherson's book *A Region Not Home*.
"Reading" is a previously unpublished letter from McPherson to an African American women's reading club in Kansas City, written circa 2010–2011.
"Junior and John Doe," "Gravitas," "Ukiyo," and "On Becoming an American Writer" first appeared in McPherson's book *A Region Not Home*.

James Alan McPherson was a short story writer and essayist. After receiving a degree from Harvard Law School, he earned his MFA in fiction from the Iowa Writers' Workshop. In 1978, he became the first Black writer to win the Pulitzer Prize for fiction. In 1981, he began teaching at the Iowa Writers' Workshop and was soon after included in the first group of artists to receive a MacArthur "Genius" Fellowship. His story "Gold Coast" is included in *Best American Short Stories of the Century*. McPherson died in 2016.

Anthony Walton is the editor and author of several books, including the nonfiction work *Mississippi: An American Journey*. His work has appeared widely in magazines, journals, and anthologies, including *The New Yorker*, *Kenyon Review*, and *Oxford American*. He is a professor and the writer-in-residence at Bowdoin College.

A NOTE ON THE TYPE

On Becoming An American Writer has been set in Caslon. This modern version is based on the early-eighteenth-century roman designs of British printer William Caslon I, whose typefaces were so popular that they were employed for the first setting of the Declaration of Independence, in 1776. Eric Gill's humanist typeface Gill Sans, from 1928, has been used for display.

Book Design & Composition by Tammy Ackerman